MW00478448

Upon This Ground I Trod
The Immigrant Journey Continues

BY PATRICK A. MORRISON, MSW

DORRANCE
PUBLISHING CO
EST. 1920
PITTSBURGH, PENNSYLVANIA 15238

The contents of this work, including, but not limited to, the accuracy of events, people, and places depicted; opinions expressed; permission to use previously published materials included; and any advice given or actions advocated are solely the responsibility of the author, who assumes all liability for said work and indemnifies the publisher against any claims stemming from publication of the work.

All Rights Reserved
Copyright © 2021 by Patrick A. Morrison, MSW

No part of this book may be reproduced or transmitted, downloaded, distributed, reverse engineered, or stored in or introduced into any information storage and retrieval system, in any form or by any means, including photocopying and recording, whether electronic or mechanical, now known or hereinafter invented without permission in writing from the publisher.

Dorrance Publishing Co
585 Alpha Drive
Pittsburgh, PA 15238
Visit our website at *www.dorrancebookstore.com*

ISBN: 978-1-6376-4394-5
ESIBN: 978-1-6376-4428-7

Upon This Ground I Trod

The Immigrant Journey Continues

CHAPTER ONE
STARTING OVER

Contract was signed, and I was officially a New York Football Giant. I was excited beyond belief that I was now a professional football player in America. The feeling took on a different "air" to it, in that I felt little more important to my community of New Rochelle and Southern Connecticut. My signing had hit the local newspapers quietly and wasn't really spoken about as much as I thought it would. I went to Al's Barber Shop to get a "shape up" that weekend and they hadn't heard of my signing at the time until I informed them. Al Sr. was excited and reminded me to touch base with Harry Carson, whom years earlier I told that I would see him in the NFL. I called all my coaches, Crocker, Mr. Bailey, and ran over to Joe's house to let him know that my signing was complete. It was an exciting time with possibilities, opportunities, as well as a "shake up" that would change my life forever.

Between May 20th and June, before rookie camp, I went back and forth from New Rochelle to New Haven to train and see Kandice. Our relationship had gone cold, not totally at its end, but due to my focus on football, training, and traveling, I hadn't spent much time with her, and we were growing apart. In spite of my neglect or lack of communication, Kandice never shut me out. She really loved me and tried desperately to keep us together. In spite of the status of our relationship, I had to remain focused on the upcoming rookie camp and do my best to come in at my best shape ever and perform like I should be there and capable. I spent the next three to four weeks working out at Iona College with Sonny and other friends who I played against in high school. "Vinny" Brunson played across town at Mt. Vernon High. He was a monster on the field, playing defensive tackle. He stood six foot five and two hundred fifty pounds of cut-up muscle. He was playing at the university a Maryland along with Big Ben who was now at the University Maryland playing offensive tackle at six nine, three hundred and thirty pounds.

Rookie camp (now called the Rookie Transition Program) would begin in mid-June for two days, before mini camp would start for the rest of the team.

Mom took the day off and drove me to Giant stadium. "We take the 95?" she said.

"Yes, Mom, exit 16."

"We go over the George Washington Bridge?"

"Yes, Ma, and then New Jersey turnpike, exit 16, Secaucus."

"It's far," she continues.

"Yes, Mom, it's far." In actuality the distance from New Rochelle to East Rutherford New Jersey is twenty-six miles. Upon arrival at he stadium, and through security, where my name was on the list to enter, I gave mom a kiss on the cheek and told her to wish me good luck. She said, "Be confident." I was directed to the locker room to put my bags down and relax. I was anxious to meet the other drafted rookies who would take the field with me that summer. The number one draft pick that year was Mark Ingram Sr. out of Michigan State, whose son now (2020) plays running back for the Baltimore Ravens. That same year was Stephan Baker, the touchdown maker, Odessa Turner, wide receiver from SW Louisiana State, and Adrian White, Safety from University of Florida. Other than Adrian, I was one of two other safeties to come into rookie mini camp. Also in camp was another free agent defensive back (corner), Wayne Haddix. Wayne was the starting corner back at Liberty Baptist University Southern who played a few months earlier where I knocked out the tight end Eric Green a few months earlier. Of course I was going to bring that up once we got started. There were about forty or so players who came in to rookie mini camp for those couple of days. We walked around the stadium and met equipment and medical personnel and position coaches. My coach was Len Fontes. The older brother of former NFL head coach Wayne Fontes of the Detroit Lions. Very personal and taught the fine points of the position. Overseeing us all on the defense was Bill Belichick, the current multi-Super Bowl champion head coach of the New England Patriots. Looking from the outside world of football, one would think that Coach Belichick was reclusive and not personable. However, in my brief encounter with him 1987, I didn't feel that way. I felt he was teacher, focused on details, spent time teaching you what he expected from you, and if you didn't get it, then he would find someone who would get it. He had a sense of humor too, even if it is was dry one. In his critique of you during film time is where his "humor" or straight disappointment in your performance for that day would be expressed the most, which frequently sequestered other players' comments, which he squashed before it got too rowdy.

After the early morning meetings, we went and picked up our practiced gear that included Nike cleats, Giant shorts, and white heavy t-shirt with the word GIANTS written across the chest. Next up was ankle taping and position film room to review the 86 season highlights. After film time, dressed in practice gear we headed out to the stadium, East Rutherford Giant Stadium. The stadium I watched for years from my living room or at Icky's house after church on Sundays. I remember walking out through the north end zone to a wide-open space of thin green artificial turf. The sun was out and the smell of professional football was in the air. After we all got to he field and admired our new home for the next two days, Coach Parcells came out to the middle of the field where we all gathered for the afternoon scheduled practice. I was in awe listening to him speak. In front of me stood the current Super Bowl champion who thought enough of me to consider drafting me and consequently signing me as a free agent. After the brief introductions of the coaching staff, we did a light stretch where the coaches would walk around and talk to you and get to know you a bit. I remember two specific coaches whose personalities I will never forget, Coach Lamar Leachman from Georgia and Jonny Parker from South Carolina; they had that southern drawl that I attempted to mimic in August of 1974. We then separated to our position coaches and work area. Coach Len Fontes was a short man with energy, encouraging the rookies not to lose the enthusiasm of being in the National Football League. One thing all coaches want to see is that player wants to be there, enthusiastic about being there, and engaged in everything that is being said by your coach. If a coach has a sense a player believes he's bigger than the team, he will be put on "Front Street" and reminded that it's a privilege to be in the NFL not a right. We then divided into two groups as we went through our back pedal drills, breaking on the ball and man-to-man techniques. I, of course, watched the techniques of the draft pick Adrian White and Wayne Haddix to see whether they looked any better or worse than myself. The best judge of that would be Coach Fontes who had a keen eye on all of us and mentioned a few times "Good job, Morrison." I thought my head would explode getting a compliment from a coach at this level. Getting a compliment from any coach at any level just ignites a level of confidence that I was to use as motivation to continue to impress on Coach Fontes and Coach Parcells.

As I made my way through the drills, all I can think about is what Sonny taught me that summer before entering Southern and the minor logistics and mechanics of playing the defensive back position. Sonny being at Southern when I got there allowed me to hone those skills to a point where it became second nature, proficient and efficient at it. Now in 1987, four years later, my skills are being recognized as sufficient enough to receive a "good job" from a Super Bowl winning defensive back coach. All of the DBs were doing well, and we all supported each other throughout the drills. After the drills, we were introduced to man-to-man coverage techniques and covering space and distance in zone coverage. This is where I focused on the other DBs to see how athletic they were and how they moved out on the field. I can honestly say the other "Big Time conference" DBs were not moving any better than me in the coverages or the drills. In fact, some of them looked stiff and breaking out of their back pedal needed more work. At that point I felt my chances of being recognized went up and a real opportunity to make the 50-man roster was a reachable. These guys weren't showing anything particularly extraordinary than what I was doing and I knew my backpedaling and breaking on the ball skills were on point. After two hours of practice, strength Coach Parker called us all back to the center of the field where Coach Parcells gave his closing remarks, stating how glad he was to see us all there, and the effort put forth. Strength Coach Parker broke us down and gave us directions of what to do next, eat lunch! Lunch was special as I recall. I believe a buffet arrangement with pasta, steaks, fish varieties, vegetables, iced tea, and soda. After filling our stomachs with a hearty brunch, we went back to watch more film reviewing defenses and the highlight film of the 1986 Super Bowl team. The highlight was more than a highlight as I viewed it. I saw it as an individual visual outline on how to play professional football. How to play football the right way with attitude, speed, anger, intelligence, and will. When I watched number 56 play and moving across the screen, it was special. Number 56 of course belonged to Lawrence Taylor, the college All-American from North Carolina, multi-all pro linebacker and unquestionably the greatest linebacker of all time. Just watching the film, you could feel the energy and tenacity coming from him and the infectious attitude projected onto his teammates. Some were more vocal than others, but for sure, Lawrence Taylor was the leader of that team on the field. Soon I would meet Lawrence Taylor (LT) and share the same space on the field with him.

After film time we were told our day was over and for those that wanted to take showers could because we a had a few moments before the buses would arrive to bring us over to our living arrangements. We gathered our things and loaded the bus. It was a typical chartered white Greyhound style bus that took us out of the stadium and headed over to the hotel. Although I've ridden in many buses as a player over my career, it felt different riding with these guys because I was now in the presence of potentially future NFL players, possibly Super Bowl champions and even a Hall of Famer. It was an exciting time for this kid 26 miles away from New Rochelle and the kid from 4,250 miles away from Paddington, England. After a short 10-15 minute ride, the bus pulled up to the Hackensack New Jersey Marriot hotel. Hackensack, SecaucusE and east Rutherford are all minor cities within 1-2 miles of each other. Many players lived near by and other neighboring cities like Jersey City. We departed the bus and checked into our rooms that were ready for us when got there. We shared rooms, and I believe my roommate was a corner back from Ohio State. Can't recall his name, but he was a personable player, had an outgoing personality, and easy to get along with. We all settled in our rooms, thinking and staying focused and mindful of our presence to not get into any trouble for the few hours we were there. "Ohio State" and me stayed in and talked football for most of the night. I called my mom to let her know how the day went. She wanted to know if I felt confident. That statement always bothered me because it made me feel that she didn't believe I felt confident in my own ability, and always left a feeling of doubt. She also asked if I ate enough. Yes to both I answered. I asked about my brother to see what he was up to. She said he was outside playing with the neighbors' kids out in the back of the building playing in the parking lot. It was getting late, so Ohio State and me turned of the lights at ten o'clock and went to bed.

The next day was the same as the first. We were picked up from our hotel early and drove the 15 minutes back to the Giants stadium. We went to our lockers and got dressed into clean washed practice gear and got our ankles taped. We then met as a team in one big film room where we were given the agenda for the day by Coach Parcells, then separated into different position conference rooms to watch more film. The DBs stayed in the same big room as the team meeting, so we didn't have to move. Coached Belichick reviewed the previous days practice film for all to see. Overall we all did well and moved with enthusiasm and intent to make plays. It was however noticeable from my perspective and I would assume from the viewpoint of coach Belichick that we all had much to work on. The timing of the NFL is real. Players are faster, and quarterbacks, if I got the beat on the ball and made a good break on it, most likely I would break up the pass, if not intercept it. My current situation showed me that it takes more than a good break on the ball and more of route recognition and anticipation. If the DB can recognize and anticipate the arrival of the ball, he has a better chance of interception than completion. That's because an NFL quarterback's ball is coming out way before the receiver has finished his pattern, and the velocity of the ball will get the ball there sooner than anticipated. I learned this firsthand. Although I made good breaks on the ball, I was one step behind or inches away from breaking up a few passes. This was my first lesson as I went against the undrafted and drafted wide receivers. I told my first experience to Rob Parker, the FOX Sports personality and writer who at the time was a sports writer for the *Daly News* paper. Rob was a classmate of mine at Southern, a couple of years older than me, who covered Southern football for the Owls newspaper. After the interview and revealing of the days practice, he wished me the best of luck and hoped I'd make it like Travis Tucker, an ex-teammate who had been drafted from Southern three years earlier to Cleveland Browns. For a small division two school, it produced some of the best in the arts, gridiron, and corporate world.

My first encounter with big time wide receivers was exciting and an eye-opening experience at the same time. Stephen Baker stood five foot eight inches and about one hundred and sixty. He was a small guy and un-assuming in his street clothes. If you were to see him on the street, you would of thought he was in his first year of high school. Fast and quick however, you learned very quickly he was not in high school and why he was in the NFL. He was so quick, I refused to go up against him by making my way to the back of the line on the other side of the field and allow another DB to go against him in one on ones and get embarrassed. His skill at running patterns with speed and quickness and his drive to catch the ball is where I learned I needed to get my game up if I want to make this team. Second up was Odessa turner; I believe he was the third pick that year to he Giants, out of NW Louisianan State University. He stood six foot three and two hundred and fifteen pounds. He was more my size, and although more physically packed than me, I took the match up as equal and at the very least a formidable challenge. As I lined up toe to toe across from Odessa on the line of scrimmage, I wanted to make sure I was in position to make a play on the ball by getting my hands on him early. I knew I was fast enough to keep up if we ran side by side, but what I couldn't let happen was allow him to get off the ball without being touched. Me getting a strike on him would be paramount. The rookie quarterbacks who came in that year were three. One was Jim Crocicchia from University Penn and the other was Mike Busch from Idaho State and another QB from a division two school. I believe the quarterback throwing was Jim Crocicchia who was a record breaking QB at the University of Pennsylvania. He was good with the short mid-range passes and a decent deep ball passer. Well, Odessa and me were up next. Snap of the ball, my hands were up ready to strike his mid section/chest area. My hands barely got there when he cleared my hands and shoved my right shoulder. "Clearing" (for the reader) is like the technique you see in the movie *The Karate Kid:* "wipe on, wipe off." Odessa "wiped off" my jab with his left and cleared me out with his left hand. Because I'm familiar with that technique, I was able to recover and get back into position and run with him down field. As we ran vigorously down the side-lines, I kept an eye on his body movement to see any kind of anticipation in his stride—none. He ran like a deer with muscles bulging out of his long arms, and I'm saying to myself "this dude is big." I was six foot three and one ninety and not overly muscular but fit. There was a significant difference in our body dimensions that became more obvious as we moved down the field. And suddenly Odessa breaks to the sidelines and extends his massive arm to keep me from closing the gap on his break. That little extension of his arm is like a mile separation on the field. I grabbed at his arm to reduce his space, but that wasn't enough. The throw from Cro-chicchia was on time, and I was but a step away and ready to make a play. I remember the ball was thrown high and outside, giving Odessa the better chance of catching the ball. I reached to knock the ball away, but I missed by inches and the ball landed in his out stretched hands, as he turned up field in one big stride heading towards the end zone. "Damn!" I yelled, as I ran to the back of the DB line. I felt some sort of way about him catching the ball on me. Every catch made is one strike against, and coming from a small school doesn't allow for too many second chances. Most power 5 school players don't think you belong amongst their brotherhood of top tier athletes, and feel they need to do extra to remind you of that. So I had to make plays, even if it was just rookie camp. The defensive backs were broken up into two groups. On the other sideline where I started on was Haddix, and he was about to be up next. Haddix played corner and safety at Liberty Baptist and was their featured defensive player in 1986. Mike Bush was the quarterback up next to throw, and he appeared to have had a stronger arm than Jim Crocicchia based from I saw during warm-up drills. He could throw the mid-level passes well and could heave it easily down the field, sixty yards on the fly. As Wayne jumped out next to take on the next receiver, you heard some rumbling as "Here we go! Lets see what you got! Touchdown maker is up." It was Stephen Baker from University of California at Fresno. His nickname was Stephen Baker, the touchdown maker. Like I said earlier, he stood five foot eight inches and one hundred and sixty pounds! And when he walked up to the line, he looked like a little child wearing his big brother's high school football uniform. His shoulder pads looked too big for him, and his face was buried in the dark crevices of his helmet. I'm saying to myself, "This guy got grafted in the third round? This kid?" Well Haddix and Baker were up next, and all eyes were on them, especially on Stephen because he was the third round pick and second receiver chosen in 1987 behind the number one pick, Mark Ingram Sr.

I remember the play like it was yesterday, and because everyone stopped what he or she was doing to watch the match up. Haddix was playing close but not too close. Stephen took a step off the line and looked back at Busch. They had a route and were on the same page. Steve got off the line of scrimmage without getting jabbed by Haddix and that was the first mistake. Now that I think back to that time, I believe we all said, "How the hell can you get your hands on that quick little guy?" Stephen ran three to five yards, leaned out towards the sidelines, and then leaned back across the middle of the field as the ball arrived as he turned his head to look for it. The quickness of his route, in and out was amazing. I was saying to myself, "I'm not going against him! I saw first hand why they called Stephen Baker the touchdown maker." With his quickness and ability to catch the ball in traffic was worth the draft money. Haddix hadn't made the play and wasn't close. There was a moderate applause from the sidelines, but of course the wide receiver line had a roaring applause for the new star Giant receiver, and it appeared the future was starting out on the right foot for the little guy. While all this was going on at one end of the field, at the other end of the field you could hear Lamar, the defensive line coach, giving the rookie linemen hell with his southern quail. "Get up, move, clear, drive now up field." The sounds, the movement on the field, the smell of Giant Stadium brought it home to me my first day. I was here! And I had made it, for now. Coach Parcells had one thing to say to Wayne about his coverage on Stephen: "you think you should get your hands on him?" Another amazing sight to see was watching Lawrence Taylor move on the field. He was six foot three and two sixty "out of shape," but it's was amazing to watch him move and rush the quarterback and watch rookie running backs try to block him. Even out of shape, Lawrence Taylor could not be touched; his speed and strength were unmatched, and to see him operate with my own eyes confirms why he's called the "greatest linebacker of all time." Rookie mini camp was finished after that. We all gathered up in he middle of the field again by Coach Parker and Coach Parcells giving the last encouraging statements that we should continue to workout stay out of trouble and be prepared for the summer. As I sat by my locker getting undressed, a sense of inadequacy came over me and it must have shown, because two seats down from mine was Phil Simms's locker. He must have seen the disappointment in my face and body and pulled up next to me and said, "Don't worry about today; put it behind you. I know how it feels coming from a small school and trying to compete, but don't let it bother you. Come back out in mini camp and be ready." Phil went to Morehead State University, a small division one school in Kentucky. First I was shocked that *Phil Simms* took time to come over and say something to this little rookie and secondly provide such encouraging words.

I wasn't sure how I was getting home because Mom was working. I called Raymond, my neighborhood high school friend, to see if he could come pick me up. He said he would but it would be later in the afternoon. "No problem, bro, see you when you get here," I said. While I waited for Raymond to get to the stadium, I sat around a little while at the stadium and hung out with a few players and getting to know them a little better. DB from Ohio State was a talkative and entertaining fellow. Fun to be around and encouraging to all the players about just doing best we can. AD wasn't around and was probably doing "draft choice" activities so I didn't get a chance to sit with him and talk about football at Florida. I sure was going to make sure I did when we returned for camp in June. As I sat there and listened and watched the remaining players awaiting their transportation to the airports, I recognized that so many young people hope and wish to be in our position to even be in the presence of other football players they may have watched on television. I recall the player who scored the last second touchdown for University of California Bears against Stanford was there too. In addition to being able to say you practiced with him on a "professional football field for a professional team" was an awesome experience. It was awesome but mind-consuming at the moment that from those great college players, only less than one percent actually makes a professional active roster. I was thankful to be there at that moment and have time to enjoy and take it all in, and not to take this opportunity for granted and I seriously understood that at anytime the opportunity can be taken away from me.

Raymond showed up around five o'clock. I couldn't be mad with him because he was doing me a favor by picking me up. Having friends available to pick me up was limited. Most of my friends were away in college. Icky went out to California after graduating from high school and hadn't returned, and I didn't know where the others that didn't play were in the neighborhood. So having Raymond available to pick me up after he got out off from work was a blessing, and I knew the ride home would be full of laughs. We got back to NewRo in forty-five minutes. We stopped at his house to chill for a minute to say hello to his mother and father. Mr. Goodlett was a five foot six, one hundred and fifty pounds of tight skin wrapped around Jamaican muscle.

Raymond's parents lineage were Jamaican and Puerto Rican. Many of Ray's jokes were cloaked with references of his aunts and uncles on both sides of his family arguing in their native tongue. Mr. Goodlett was a blue color worker who provided a great beautiful home for his family. Mrs. Goodlett was the home keeper that didn't play and made sure the "young people knew their place and acted that way." As I sat on the plastic-covered couch, I made sure I didn't touch anything. Mrs. Goodlett always knew if something was moved from where she placed it in the living room. She would come out from the kitchen and engage in small talk looking you over to make sure you were sitting appropriately on her couch and nothing was moved. When Mrs. Goodlett left the room after Raymond returned from his room upstairs (where none of his friends were allowed,) he would ask, "Did my mom come in here?" If you said yes, he would ask, "What she want?" He usually knew what she wanted, but it was way of having your back and putting you at ease and letting you know that she does that to everyone. "Let's be out," Ray said as we headed out the front door. I lived on the south end of NewRo, up town and a few blocks from Main Street, and around the corner from my high school teammate Mitchell Bartee who was killed down the street from the bank where Icky's mom would pick me up for school and where Raymond worked on his third shift job. Raymond worked for NBW Bank sorting checks, mail, and transporting documents to companies located in the World Trade Center buildings in Manhattan. During my senior year in high school and before I went off to college, Raymond would pick me up at 12 A.M. at my building on North Ave and we would head into the city together. It was always blast because he would pull

15

up like he was about to take off in a drag race in his little white Ford Escort company car. I would jump in and off we went on 95 south laughing about some crazy event that happened to him that day or some crazy interaction he had with his girlfriend Rene that day. I think it was his moment to get things off his chest and relax with his boys. On the way back from his run into Manhattan, we would stop off on 125th Street and head over to Sylvia's restaurant to get a late night/early morning breakfast meal before we headed home providing more laughter as Raymond kept the midnight shift ladies laughing over some grits, bacon, and chicken.

"Thanks, bro" as we pulled up to 311 North Ave, my apartment building.

I said, "I'll get with you later."

"You rolling with me tomorrow tonight?" Ray asked.

"I don't think so. I gotta chill with Mom and Pops and tell them about my camp."   "Peace!" Raymond said, as he was sped away back home. I had my backpack and a suitcase in hand as I ran up to our fifth floor apartment, 12B. I had my key so I let myself in. I called out but no answer. It was six o'clock now, and I knew that if Mom wasn't home by this time it only meant she went to her second job at the nursing home where she worked as an aide to the elderly. During the day, Mom worked for the board of education as a lunch provider. She was the "Lunch Lady", and at night as a nurses aid. As I squeezed into my ten by five (10x5) bedroom and put my bags on my bed (if I put them on the floor I couldn't walk to my desk and window), I walked the few feet and looked out my window, down North Ave watching the hustling and bustling of the streetcars and pedestrians running and dodging each other as to make their way to their destinations on time. It was good to be home and in my own bed, in our own small apartment, with the noise and yelling of the occupants downstairs. I wasn't sure where my brother was when I got home. He usually came home and stayed at the neighbors' house one floor down or Mr. and Mrs. Roach's house on the first floor that had an older daughter who would watch him until someone came home first. But who that person was depended on what sport season I was in, if Mom was working or if "Dad" was available and in the "right" state of mind. I know it was a struggle for Mom to manage two boys and a husband battling alcohol addiction. She never complained about her situation, but I knew it was a heavy burden. I remember coming home from school one day and found burned-out cigarettes in a plate when I got home and Mom was sitting on her bed acting busy. I was in so much shock that I couldn't even ask her if she was smoking. I knew it wasn't my Dad's because he wasn't home and you could still smell the fresh nicotine in the air. Our situation was challenging to say the least, and because I recognized our limited resources and the strain on Mom, it pushed me to do what I could do by making the team and releasing some of that burden of her shoulders.

It was roughly nine o'clock when the door opened and my dad walked through the door. He noticed I was in my room and said, "You're here?"

"Yeah, I came home a few hours ago. Raymond bought me home," I said.

"They let you go," he said. I said yes Dad, this was a short stay but we go back to camp next month again. "Again?" he said. "They didn't make up their mind yet?" Dad always asked or provided a quirky comment, but I knew he was playing and pushing me to think and look at my situations from all sides. As I lay back down he asked if I was hungry.

I said "not really."

He said, "There's some food in here if you want it." When he said that, my ears went up like Icky's German shepherd because I knew if he brought food home, that there was a masterpiece waiting for me in the kitchen. Dad was a master chef who worked at a few country clubs as the lead chef. Unfortunately for his struggles, his tenor at these clubs was frequently interrupted. For now however I wasn't going to think about that; I was going to enjoy the spread that awaited me in the kitchen. We had curried rice, multiple mixed peppers, onions, strip steak, and cabbage with a sauce. Great is an understatement. His cooking always satisfied my palate. His along with Mom's cooking were always enough to fill my belly. Even though I ate well, I still had a difficult time gaining weight. I tried by eating all these wonderful meals, but it never stuck. I was full after the big meal that went down wonderfully with some " red" Kool-Aid, and I was ready to hit the hay for the rest of the night. As I settled in my room, putting my bags on the floor to make room for me to jump in, I heard Dad call my name. " Pat?"

"Yes, Dad?" I said.

As I got up from my bed, he met me at my door and said "here" as he gave me a little brown bag.

I asked him, "What's in it?"

He said, "If you ask another question, nothing for you." I looked inside the bag and in it was what he's always had done when he came home late from work. He would bring my favorite chocolate candy, a Kit Kat bar. He always acted indifferent to things, but actions like this, as small as it may seem, I knew he cared about my mom and me. I jumped on my bed, turned on my black and white TV, and ate my Kit Kat, good night.

CHAPTER TWO
GROWING UP

I woke up as I heard the door open. It was mom who just returned home from her second job at the nursing home down on Pelham Ave on the southwest side of New Rochelle. It was about 11:45 P.M. when she came in, and I could hear her bags shuffling alongside her body as she struggled to get everything inside the apartment. I jumped out of bed calling her name to let her know I was home and to greet her with a kiss, provide a helping hand, and I was anxious to tell her about my three days at rookie camp. I could tell she was tired so I didn't want to overwhelm her with details, so I waited until the morning when we could talk more with clear minds. Mom worked hard, and I don't know how she did it when I think back on that period in our lives. A few times in high school and when she would come to see me in college, she would leave her job at the nursing home, run to the hospital and do her overnight duty, then wake up and drive to the high school or whatever school she was to asked to work at that week, and sometimes sleep in the parking lot for an hour or two before she would go in and prepare the meals for the day. She had three jobs and still found time to drive me back to school. I guess she saw the excitement in my eyes and heard the tone of my voice and wanted to know more about recent experience. All I ever wanted to was to please Mom because of where she has come from to where she was today. Then she asked me, "You feel confident?" Again, that statement. It never sat well with me, because all that I've done up to that point from Pop Warner, to high school, college, and now having an opportunity in the NFL, why I'm I still being asked if I "feel confident." Have I not proven myself yet? Hasn't my play over the years proven that I'm confident to go up against other men and beat them at the game where the fastest, strongest, and those whose will I have out dominated and outperformed? "Yes, Ma, I felt confident; we can talk more in the morning. Goodnight."

I woke up to the aroma of a Caribbean feast! Dad always made great food for us. I jumped out of bed and ran into the kitchen to see what he put together. He was sitting there with his legs crossed reading his *New York Post* newspaper. He was so British. Although he was born in Jamaica, he spent much of his adulthood in London where he honed his craft as a businessman and chef. He made history by becoming the first black man to own a pub in Oxford right outside out of London. "You wash up," he said as he saw me approaching he stove.

"Nah, not yet, I just wanted to see what you made." It was everything! I didn't even know we had this much food in the house to be cooked.

He said, "Go wash up, and I'll have your plate ready." After my shower I did my hair, which included some Murray's Grease and Vaseline lotion, and I was ready to eat! I made my way quickly to the kitchen where the table was empty.

"What's up, Dad?"

"In here," as he called me into the combined dining and living room area, where on the table was a feast set for a king. He made ackee and salt fish, cabbage mixed with all the colorful peppers, dumplings, fried fish with the heads still on, plantains, and of course a side of bacon. I was ready to get it started because it was a while since I was away at school and enjoyed a good home-cooked meal. Mom made her way out of the back room as she was getting my brother together. He was about nine now and getting big and full of adventure. He sat with me as I filled Mom in on the last couple days in New Jersey. She attended my games in college as often as she could and not because she actually understood what was happening on the field, but she attended just to support me and be there knowing that it's was just us making it through this world as immigrants, where oftentimes Mom would tell me stories of her growing up and the games she played with her siblings and cousins as children with little to know equipment. She knew the American game was rough and different to anything she ever knew before, but she believed you had to be confident in yourself that you can do it because no one will help you reach your goal but yourself. As me, my brother, and mother sat at the table and ate the gourmet meal and discussed my activities at rookie camp, Dad made his way back to the kitchen and returned to reading his newspaper. That's what he did all the time, work, read, cook, and drink. I told Mom I would be heading back to New Haven tomorrow, Sunday. Kandice didn't come to many of my games either. She spent most of her time at cosmetology school and in the hair salon in downtown New Haven. She was widely recognized as one of the best in New Haven and Connecticut to "do hair." I missed my graduation day because I was home for the draft, but I needed to get back to train and see Kandice before I headed off to mini camp in June. She said, "Okay, be careful and will I see you before you go?" "yes mom" I said.

It was a bright Saturday morning, and what most of us did to catch up on the latest sports and drama in the city was to head over to Al's barbershop to get a fresh cut and talk sports. I walked in, and salutations around the shop were handed out. I felt little important this time around. Mr. Holmes Sr., the owner of the shop, was a soft-spoken man that was engaging and spoke to all the kids growing always with an encouraging word towards us to do well. As I took a seat and waited my turn, he said to me, "Your friend just left."

I said, "Who? Harry Carson?"

"Yes," Mr. Holmes said. I was hoping I would catch him because months before I told him that I would see him in the league, and months later here I am, going to be his teammate in a couple of weeks. It was an exciting and conflicting time for me. I know I was chosen as one of the best in the country to play this game called football, but I also understood that only a select few would be given the opportunity to put on their team jersey and wear it full time. My time had come and it was time to show up and show out or leave it alone. I got my Philly high fade top haircut working. In 1987, the high top fade was in and I had curly black hair so it looked "cool" once I put all together and I couldn't go back looking raggedy heading back to New Haven. I was a professional football player now, who just signed with the New York Football Giants, and received his bonus check of a few thousand dollars, which was more than I or my mother had seen in a single six month period, ever. So to pull up to campus not looking the part would not be a good look. After my haircut and pleasantries were passed around as I was leaving, I wasn't sure where to go. During this time, most of my friends were still in school and weren't home yet. Icky hadn't moved back from California yet and was living the good life working on some TV shows and just working the streets, so I thought I would see him before I went back.

I decided to head up to Iona College first. By this time Coach Crocker was the head and first football coach of Iona College. He brought along with him a few of the high school coaches and players with him to get the program off to a good start. Angelo, who I played with high school and against in college from American International, was an assistant DB coach under our high school coach, Coach Capellan who coached NewRo high school girls' track and still does to this day, the DBs. He also hired our high school offensive line coach, Rich D'Amico, and my high school quarterback Bill Barrett was on the staff too. He had just finished playing wide receiver at the University of New Hampshire and was attending Iona to complete his master's. Coach was gathering a team of men who he knew were good men of character, who new football and had a history of winning. I figured I would stop by and see how things were going. Iona College was about one and half miles on the north end of town, down the street from the high school. Many times people would drive by Iona and think NewRo High was the college and Iona the high school. Iona was a well-established small Catholic university, which had a strong business program. It's a very successful program where many of its graduates find jobs on Wall Street or in high-level Manhattan companies in general. I went to the football office and I found coach there behind his desk. It was good to see him as we hugged and congratulated each other on our new endeavors and positions. We talked football for about an hour or so as he told me about the program and the competition at the division 3 levels they've been playing in for past two years. After catching up with "croc," it was time for me to leave when coach said, "If there's there's anything I can do for you, just let me know." Those were comforting words coming from my former coach who helped mold me into the man I would become. He tolerated my "quirkiness" but never has forsaken me nor given up on me. Little did I know at the time I would need him to open opportunities in this game called football again.

Wasn't much left to do since no one was around so I headed back home and stopped by Goufmans convenient store on North Ave. I picked up a box of jungle juice and went home. I remember it was a quiet day actually and it felt kind of weird. It was weird in a way that; as I looked around the city and watched the hustle and bustle, I recognized people really didn't care or knew much of any of my achievement towards the NFL. People have their own aspirations, ambitions, and basic life expectations and are just trying to get through another day alive. I was still playing a game, and although playing football would be "my job," it still was a game and not ditch-digging hard labor, saving lives, or building anything. It is just a game. When I got home, I packed my suitcase for my trip back to Connecticut on Sunday. I still had to move out of my of campus apartment on Fitch Street where I had two weeks left before the summer students would be moving in. I told Mom what my plans were for Sunday and that I would take Metro North into New Haven. She said she's off and that she would drive me and bring back home whatever she could. Dad wasn't around when I got homes, but usually on the weekends he would be working at the country clubs so I wasn't expecting him to be available. While staring out of my bedroom window, another one of those NewRo thoughts came across my mind and how my life got to where it is. I thought back to my first days on Washington Ave as I looked left out my window towards the hospital where I would cut through to go Columbus Elementary School, then to looking up North Ave towards the high school were I experienced some of the greatest people who changed my life. I had nearly forgotten the little things about New Rochelle that made it special by being away for the past four years in Connecticut. That night I ate another great meal of baked chicken, mashed potatoes, gravy and calaloo with carrots. Mom said she would run to the store and pick up a few things to take back with me. My plan was to stay at Kandice's parents' home and with her. This would allow us to reconnect, while I continued working out and get ready to leave in June. I slept well Saturday night. I watched my usual favorite shows, *Saturday Night Live* and *Benny Hill*. Tomorrow would be a new day and the continuation of the dream that would ultimately put me in place that I would never expect to be at twenty-two years old.

Sunday morning, up and early, sun is bright and the skies are blue. I smell bacon cooking in the kitchen and that tells me Mom is up and I need to get my things together. I took a shower then headed to kitchen to see what was on the table. There were dumplings, eggs, more calaloo, and ackie. Heaven! My bags were packed and ready to go. Mom worked hard, and by my senior year in college she bought herself a nice 1985 Blue Pontiac Bonneville. It was our first decent car that we ever owned. Her first car was a gigantic, 1978 red Ford something. Not sure what kind of Ford it was. It just said FORD on the trunk. It was but it was huge! The next car she purchased was when I was in high school, a green Grenada, which I "took out" some nights while Mom was sleeping and headed over to Icky's or Raymond's house. We would go into the city to Hunts Point and bother the prostitutes or just hang out on the block for a while with the fellas, Butch, Alamo, Terry, and the fair-weather brothers, Colin and Tony.

We gathered our things and prepared for our way down the five floors to the packed blue Bonneville. Mom had a bag in her hand. I asked her, What's in the bag?"

She said, "Some food to help you gain weight." I peeked in and saw that she bought a big slab of steak. It was enough steak to last me for a month! I was like, "Mom, that's a lot!"

She smiled and said, " How ya gonna bounce da man dem if ya weak?" We both smiled as we carried on down the stairs. Our apartment building was right next to Interstate 95, so it was easy to get on and off I-95. However Southern is on the Hutchinson River Merritt Parkway side so we would have to drive a couple of blocks north on North Ave and get on interstate 15, the Hutch. As we drove down North Ave, I looked out the window and day dreamed of all the significant people, places, and memories that helped me on this journey. Goufman's, Al's, Coligni Ave with the fellas, The Winthrop Ave "Jets", The Ape Yard, City Hall, the hollow and the high school. About a quarter mile up from the high school was the Hutch, and that's were we got on headed to Connecticut. Mom liked driving to Connecticut because it was a time for her to get away from work and spend time with me, and "visit." Whenever she traveled either with her church or with friends and family it was always an adventure, and unfortunately, the adventure between us frequently ended with us arguing with each other about her driving. Mom's driving was an adventure, and sometimes I wasn't sure if we would make it to our destination or not. Thank goodness for Raymond who came through a couple of times. If Mom missed an exit, she would stop, back up on the highway to the exit, and then get off. It was hair-raising to say the least. But we always made it to Southern, angry, but we made it. Mom liked driving into New Haven from the Merritt Parkway to Exit 59. It was the exit to get off for Southern, and as you approached the exit there was the West Rock Tunnel. The tunnel was her landmark that told her she had arrived to her destination. "We almost there," she would say, "my exit, exit 59."

We arrived in New Haven and went to my apartment first to pack up my things. I didn't have much, no fan, no microwave, none of those things students have these days. All I had fit into a standing four-foot high by two-foot wide suitcase. After I packed up, we left the Fitch Street apartments and heading back towards West Hills where Kandice lived. It was a blue collar, hard working neighborhood on the fringes of the West Hills Projects. It was a tough part of West Hills where often you would hear sirens of police and ambulance cars throughout the night. We got to the home where Mr. and Mrs. Jones, and Kandice, her brothers George and Steven, and younger Sister Wendy lived. Kandice's older brother George was away in the Army, and Wendy was home and getting ready to graduate from a tier-one college institution in the south. Mrs. Jones and Mom had the same name, Jean, so they hit it off pretty good. They were happy to see each other again after two years, and Mom thanked Mrs. Jones for allowing me to stay the remainder of the summer in their home while I trained. We unpacked the steaks and put them in their freezer to stay frozen. I felt kind of weird having my food in their refrigerator. It felt like college: "This is my food and do not touch it" written on tape, taped across the container. The Joneses weren't rich people. But they were loving, mild mannered, and caring. They put everything into their four children to keep them safe from the West Hills Projects' influence and to live productive lives. Although they never asked, I made sure to let them know if they wanted some steaks they should feel free, but politely they refused.

Mom stayed for a bit and conversed with the Jones family while Kandice and I found a place to put my standing suitcase and an empty draw to put my things in and to settle down. Mom left about an hour later, jumped on the Merritt Parkway around the corner from the house, and headed back home to NewRo. It was a long day, but it was good to be settled in and relaxed for the night and get ready to start working out in the morning. Kandice had always told me of a dirt path that led from her neighborhood and through the woods, which would eventually bring to a park opening at the base of West Rock. The park opening would be around the corner from the Farnham Ave of Southern's campus where I could finish the rest of my workout at the school gym. I thought that was a good idea to take that route instead of running the hard pavement of the streets, and I would possibly get more out of running through a challenging terrain by working on my balance and agility.

After a good night's rest, I was up early and ready to go for my morning run through the wooded path towards campus. Running through the woods felt like a scene from one of those scary movies being chased or the feeling that someone is watching you. The path was winding and steep in some parts, which forced me to adjust the speed and angles of direction. I had to jump high over tree limbs that fell over time or during the latest storm, or bend low under them while running through the wooded land-scape. This part of the training would definitely help in my agility, which I would need when trying to cover players like Stephen Baker or Mark Engram. I made it through the woods, which came out to an opening on the other side of the mountain unto a soft-ball field. I passed this field many times while in school but never knew there was a path leading through it to West Hills. Kandice said she took it couple of times during the day when she would come see me on campus but walked the long way on the streets around the park when she would come see me at night. The run down and through the woods was about a mile long stretch, then Kandice would run sometimes on the weekends if her schedule allowed. I never liked lifting weights, but I knew it was a necessary evil that I had to confront if I wanted to compete effectively on the next level. I didn't mind benching, but I despised squatting even more. No one was in the gym so I started to get to it on my own. I did the best I could, but you never really reach your max-imum workout without someone pushing you to do more, some-thing I learned from the many years at Southern under Gilbride and Cavanaugh. When you think you can't do another one hun-dred yard dash, you soon realize you have two or three more left in you. Pushing through your perceived maximum is a psycho-logical battle that athletes have to face many times and overcome to be successful. Being able to push what he or she "thinks" they can maximize when in reality there is much more within them-selves. Well, I pushed as much as I could on the bench without breaking my neck. I wouldn't do more than two hundred and twenty-five pounds more than eight to ten times, because by the time I got to ten, the weight started to become too difficult and my arms begin to buckle. Pushing myself to do more without a spot could be fatal. After a couple of sets in the weight room, I was done, and so I headed out to get lunch at "Hattie's," the diner on the corner of Fitch and Blake street at the bottom of campus. The next day was the same schedule: get up early and run through the woods and down to campus. But on this day I would do ad-ditional speed work by doing ten one-hundred-yard dashes for stamina and ten forty-yard dashes for burst of speed. I would fol-low this schedule for the next four weeks, along with eating my steaks and potatoes and whatever else the Jones family were of-fering up at dinnertime. I did as much preparation as I could to be ready for Giant mini camp on June 19th, 1987.

There was a disappointing moment I experienced while in New Haven during my time there. School had just commenced for the year, but there were still a few students around campus either working or packing up their last minute essentials to take home. I ran into Rhonda Jefferson. Rhonda was a class below me but was well liked and known around campus as a leader and friend to most all the students and administration. We saw each other on campus as I was walking towards the field house and she called me over to say hello and wish me good luck. As we spoke about things regarding me, our mutual friends and other students and what her plans were for the summer, she said, "I have to tell you something about your 'friend,' but you can't say anything."

The way she said it made me uneasy because now I wanted to know what made her so uneasy to want to tell me this information that had to be kept to myself and not to be shared with *anyone*. Before she would tell me, I had to promise her I wouldn't say anything to the person, so I promised. Rhonda told me that a close teammate told her in a disparaging way that "He's not gonna make the team!" referring to me. She said he said it in a way that showed he didn't support or even had confidence in me to make the team. What she disclosed really threw me for loop because I thought my friends and teammates over the past four years were men of integrity where we cried, fought, and bled together on the gridiron. Even if the person didn't think I would make the team, I would think they would want me to be successful or just wish me all the best. Well I recognize then that not all people want for you what they want for themselves. People can be selfish, envious, and downright mean, but I know God has the last answer and he is the best planner and has the best reward for me. I took that negativity to heart at the time and took the pain of that statement to use as I had used my pain before to overcome my humble beginnings, my abuse, and direct it to whomever I would run into when I got to camp. Rhonda was offended too. She said what was said was "hate" and she too was disappointed that it was said and in who said it. She offered me comfort with kind words and hope and wishing me all the best to make the team.

My time in New Haven was running out, and soon it was time to get back home and prepare for camp. I was thankful for Kandice and her family for having me in their home and an opportunity for us to strengthen our relationship. Our relationship by this time was strained because while in school we had some difficult moments that brought these strains on. Kandice however still supported me the best she could by asking her parents to have me stay for the couple weeks in their home while I was there in New Haven. Our future would be in question, but for now, I had other things on my mind that I needed to focus on, and anything else would be an additional strain on me, and a hindrance to my objective. I returned home about a week before camp and took the Metro North train home to our apartment, which was about one hundred yards down the street.

Time was drawing near, and honestly I was scared to death. It had been a while since a New Rochelle player had been to the NFL. The last one was Calvin Whitfield who played running back and defensive back at the University of Rhode Island who graduated in 1983. He went on to play for Montreal Alouettes of the Canadian Football League and the Buffalo Bills of the NFL. Before him was George Stark, offensive lineman for the Washington Redskins. I was next in the lineage of New Rochelle football players to have a shot of making an active roster, and attending mini camp would be my next stop to fulfill the NewRo football lineage and living out my dream. My suitcase had wheels on it so I rolled home and lugged my stand-up suitcase up to the fifth floor. I opened the door and found Mom home. She had arrived earlier from church and was resting in her room. For the next week I made my rounds around town to see friends. Went to Icky's house, he was home now, so I got a boost of support and confidence from him. He always kept me up with positive "nouns" with no filter. His attitude was "Fuck 'em, Hollywood." Hollywood was the name I was called in high school by my teammates based on the theatrics and animation of my play on the field. When I left Icky's house, I felt on top of the world like I could do this. I stopped by Coligni Ave to see Raymond and his family. His father was home, and he was a man of few words. Raymond told him I was off to play for the Giants! His response was "Oh yea, good luck," and he went into his kitchen. Raymond and I looked at each other and laughed. Raymond tried to impress upon him that it was the "pros." He said, "Oh yea, good luck." Mr. Goodlett wasn't easily impressed, but I know he wished the best for me. Between my visits I continued training by running the streets and going to Iona to lift. None of the familiar faces were around, but I did my best to stay pumped and not lose any of the advances I had previously made in New Haven. By Saturday I was ready to go. I was anxious, excited, and scared with anticipation. Tomorrow, Sunday, June 19th, 1987 would be the day I've been waiting for since August 1974.

CHAPTER THREE
SHOWTIME

I believe Mom drove me to mini camp bright and early on Sunday morning, but I am not one hundred percent sure. Back then she was comfortable driving and would drive everywhere. She would drive the church van to events upstate New York and over to Sherwood Island Park Beach in Rye, New York. I remember it being a sunny June day in Pleasantville, New York on the campus of Pace University. Pace University is a small suburban state university in Westchester, New York with a fully accredited curriculum with majors from liberal arts to engineering. The day had finally arrived, and I, with my one suitcase in hand, was ready as can be to meet and hit the field with the 1986 NFL Super Bowl Champions. Our accommodations were in he dormitories on campus and we would have a training table too. This was a far cry from what I was used to at Southern Connecticut. The training table at Southern was Connecticut Hall where the entire student body ate, and you better be there early before the food service lines shut down at 6-6:30 P.M. At the time, Southern didn't have an alternative eating hall or building for food after hours. It was either you ate at Conn Hall or you were out of luck for the evening. The food served for lunch was the food of champions, for example: spaghetti and meatballs, salads, meat choices, drinks, and sweets… You had to be disciplined though, especially the linemen because there were rules and expectations that had to be met regarding weight for players to adhere to, if they wanted to play or get paid. My roommate would be Wayne again. It was good seeing him, but I knew as rookies and the limited roster he would be my competition going into camp. We then headed over to the field and locker rooms where the equipment was being handed out. I remember my locker being next to Adrian. He was put together like a pit bull and had the demeanor of lion ready to pounce on you. He was engaging but conservative and like a silent storm about to erupt.

I was given two pairs of footwear, high-top Nike cleats and low Adidas. Our practice dress was a white Giants undershirt, Giants shorts, socks, and my new jersey. For four years I wore the number forty-eight (48), and I believed I left an imprint on the gridiron at Southern with that number that will never be forgotten. My new number would be thirty-seven (37), a regular number with no history and no name associated with it. It would be up to me to be noticed and to have number 37 leave an imprint in he minds of my peers and the Giants coaching staff. My biggest thrill was when I received my helmet. The color was a deep navy blue with the word GIANTS written on the side of it. This was my biggest moment. If I was sent home tomorrow I would be happy to say I had my own New York Football Giants helmet. After the sizing up and handing out of all the equipment, we headed out to the field for some stretching, running around, and position drills. Monday will be the first official practice day where everyone would be battling for a team roster spot. In the defensive back group, we were all there together, and finally I could see, assess, and evaluate my position and probability of making the team. After looking at the full defensive backfield, I became a little disillusioned at what I saw. The returning starters at safety were Terry Kinnard and Kenny Hill. Both were the starting safeties last year on the Super Bowl team. Their back-ups were Herb Welch and the guy I didn't want to play behind when being recruited out of high school and who was the safety at the University of Pittsburgh, Tom Flynn. "I can't shake this guy," I said to myself. Tom played for the Green Bay Packers and was cut in the middle of the 1986 season but later picked up by the Giants, and he played good enough for them to resign him. So I began to count, "That's four right there, plus Adrian, makes five, then me six." No way were they gonna keep six safeties. So I felt that I couldn't control my situation and all I could do was "to be my best and leave unto the lord the rest." The corners were Marc Collins, Perry Williams, Elvis Patterson, Greg Lasker, and Haddix who they moved to Corner. Doug Smith (Ohio State) was there too, so we all were fighting for a spot somewhere on the team. Most rookies are in this situation, and the best they can do is hopefully doing enough to make the special teams roster with the hopes of future opportunities and overall adjusting to the NFL system. Well I had my hands full in attempting to break through this maze of obstruction, but I would give a great try. As we met in our position groups I could feel the "divide" between rookies and veterans from the first day. Usually when you're new on the block you want to show enthusiasm and step up in the line by taking the initiative and paying close attention. Well what I felt was, "sit back, wait your turn, and pay attention." Which was understandable because I didn't know what I was supposed to do and the protocol and the process of things to come. As we went through the back peddling and breaking on the ball drills on our section of the field, I could hear Leachman on the far end of the field and a scramble of noise throughout he practice. We weren't doing any major activities like play running or hitting, but catches were being made by beautifully thrown balls by Sims, Hostetler, and even Crocihiccia. A good relaxing first morning day of practice, which ended up just like it did in rookie camp with Johnny Parker bringing us to the middle of the field and Coach Parcells having the last words. After practice we all walked towards the locker room as fans stood along the fence line waiting for the team to leave the field. You could hear the fans yell out the names of those players you would hear ever Sunday afternoon: "LT," "Joe," "Phil," and so on. I wasn't expecting anyone to ask for mine because no one knew who I was yet. But it was really cool to see the fans all around the fence line watching and waiting for us to leave the field. I could not stick around and hope some kid would ask for my autograph, I had somewhere to go. We had dinner and then a team meeting, then defensive position meeting where the football staff would be handing out the defensive play books, then lastly, special teams meeting.

The defensive playbook was about four to five inches thick. My anxiety level rose after getting it in my hands because it reminded me of my freshman year at Southern and I had to learn the playbook there. Safety has to make all the calls to get everyone lined up right and at Southern my first year was a challenge. In spite of that, I felt okay because safety was like home-cooked food. We were told to return to our rooms and study the first two coverages in the 5-inch playbook and come tomorrow ready to play. The first one was Cover Zero and the other, Cover One. The first being a zone and the second being man-to-man coverage. Back in the room Haddix and I got to it studying our positions. To my surprise, the position I was told to learn was the Strong Safety Position and not Free Safety. At Southern I played Free Safety, which is considered the quarterback of the defense. In *Before Common Ground, Living the American Dream: The Journey of an Immigrant Football Player*, I outline my journey to solidifying the Free Safety position and the great detail put forth to be pretty good at that position. Now my position was changed to Strong Safety, which felt like I was starting all over again, and this time I didn't have two years to get it down. I had less than four weeks before the first pre-season game. I was able to get about an hour and half of studying in before Coach Sweatman, the assistant defensive back and special teams coach, came knocking at our door and said, Light's outs, men." Well, I thought to myself that I shouldn't worry and just pay attention, listen and go full speed in practice. There were two practices a day, and the next day we got up bright and early and hit the field around ten o'clock. The fans were out early to meet and greet us again at the wired fence with applause and support for another great year to come. I felt like I was part of he 1986 Super Bowl team, because the fans cheered everyone and wanted everyone's autograph. When LT hit the field it was like the president came to town, and the fans went into a frenzy and crazy. " LT, LT, LT, LT!" is all you heard. I understand completely, and I found myself saying, "LT" as I ran out unto the field unnoticed. It was a great moment, and feeling the energy in the air of the fans and knowing the 1987 season would soon be here with hopes and dreams of another run at the Super Bowl. After breaking into our positions, Coach Fontes and Sweatman ran us through our drills. I sat back and watched the veterans as they moved and interacted with each other. You could see the coordination and parallel movements in their strides as they broke out of their back peddles to forty-five degree angles, up and back. You could see the teamwork come together after playing with each other for a while. Kenny Hill, a Yale University graduate, was quiet, but he was the silent leader. Terry Kinard was a little more outgoing, talkative, and a jokester who kept the group loose. I was up next, and vaguely recall that I was going with, but I believe it was the DB from Ohio State, Doug Smith. One thing I knew how to do well was my back peddling and breaking techniques on the ball, backward and forwards. The skills instilled in me by Sonny my freshman summer coming into Southern, Coach Bush my first DB coach, and Southern had done a great job in teaching me the fundamentals of being a defensive back which was basically being able to walk backwards as good as I could walk forwards with balance and stability. Well I could do that, as Coach Fontes said, "Good job, Morrison." After drills we were split up on both sides of the field, the same way were split up during one-on-ones at mini camp earlier in the summer. I thought I was more prepared now than I was in rookie camp. I understood better the physicality, speed, and environment of the NFL. It's not only the physical ability that allows you to be successful on this level of competition, but there is also a mental toughness component that goes along with the later. The DBs started doing one-on-ones amongst ourselves. There was no pressure to perform at the moment. Time was allotted before we faced the wide receivers to warm up and fine-tune our man on man technique. I was up next to run the pattern against the DB. Up with me to warm up was Elvis (Toast) Patterson who was a veteran DB out of the University of Kansas. He stood about 5'11, and looking at his arms he was strong. Watching him in warm-ups, you can see he had quick feet and speed to match. I was next to run a simple down and out route at twelve yards. Crocihiccia who was throwing said, "Hike.," As I was about to take off the line, Elvis gave me a two-hand strike to my chest plate which sent a shiver down my spine. I looked at him like he was crazy, like "Yo! We're on the same side of the ball getting warmed up." He saw the look on my face and made it clear rookie that "you gotta be ready." Point taken, I said to myself. I was held up at the line, so we tried again after the first attempt. I heard Coach Belichick yell over, "Let's go over there! What's the hold up?" So I was up again and able to get off the ball this time with the "wipe on, wipe off" technique. I ran the route but wasn't able to get away from "Toast," and he undercut the route and intercepted the ball. I felt defeated even though it was warm-up and I wasn't a professional wide receiver. It was good defeat though because it was a learning moment where I got to see live the ability of an NFL DB, even if he was a "seasoned" DB like "Toast." I realized even a veteran DB was better than the best college DB. When it was my turn, I played the off technique, which was playing back off the receiver about 7 yards deep. I don't remember who I went up against, but I remember the ball going incomplete and me running back to the back of the line with the ball and threw it back to the quarterback line. The whistle blew, and there was and uproar coming from the other side of the field. It was time to do one-on-ones with the wide receivers. Our group moved to the other side of the field and lined up against a mix of tight ends and running backs. When it was my turn, I hadn't received the luck of the draw; I didn't go against a rookie tight end. I got the hand that had me going up against Mark Bavaro. Mark was one of the two great tight ends the 1986 Super Bowl champion Giants had on their roster, and the other being Zeke Mowatt. Mark was quiet, and to this day, I don't remember ever hearing him speak. I lined up in front of him about five yards of the ball. When the ball was snapped, he looked like a big bear coming at me. Mark was about six feet five inches and two hundred and six pounds of sold muscle. As he came closer towards me, I got back into my perfect and confident back pedal watching him close the gap between us. When he got within arms distance, I outstretched my hands and kept him at a distance giving myself room to maneuver if necessary to change direction. He put an outside move then a sharp inside move up field. That move didn't shake me, and I was all over him like a blanket. I think he must of thought I was too "all over him like a blanket" because he got upset as he couldn't get loose of me as the ball sailed over both our outstretch arms, incomplete. He complained by his look at me, as though he was about to confront me, as our eyes connected. He didn't, as his demeanor deflated as he picked up the ball and ran back to he offensive huddle. When I returned to the back of the DB line, I received some pats on my back and the butt and words of congratulations. Part of me felt good with my first time up and I hoped to continue with these little successes, but the other half of me was scared as shit as my legs felt like spaghetti.

By Wednesday afternoon practice, Special Teams Unit was implemented and that was run by Coach Romeo Carnell and assisted by Coach Sweatman. I really liked Coach Romeo because he would tell me that I was doing a good job and for me to keep it up and what I needed to do to stay ahead of the curve of what would be coming. I was one of the inside sprinters attackers to the ball. I believe the Giants looked at me as a hitter, that getting me in the mix would be their objective. I didn't mind because I was going to give it my all and lay it all out on the line if I had to. I didn't believe however I was strong enough to take the constant pounding on my body being hit by these guys weighing two hundred plus pounds and running 4.4, 4.5 forty yard dash sprints. Well, if I wasn't living up to their expectations, Romeo would let us know, which made you keenly aware of how close you were to the curve. Special teams is the first and last place a rookie has the opportunity to show and make the 52-man roster, so if anything else, I had someone with whom I could gage my progress. As the day began to wind down, you could tell the team was getting more adjusted to camp and becoming comfortable with each other. You got to see the group dynamics between the seasoned veterans like Harry Carson and Joe Morris, and younger players like Mark Collins, Kinard, and of course the rookies. Some veterans were more welcoming than others, and then there were those and a particular defensive lineman that just had a nasty distant attitude towards rookies. I picked that up immediately and made it my purpose to stay away from him. Not because I was scared of him or of retaliation but because I knew I still had this underlying anger and temperament that would explode on anyone and him; win or lose there would be a problem. Generally we all got along and worked hard off on the field to secure a spot for the 1987 season. By Saturday the rookies had enough of the defense to go against the offense and run plays and for coaches to evaluate the players. There are three particular plays I remember during this time, during "team" portion of practice and I was out at the strong safety position, the position I was still getting used to, but I was out there on the third team behind Kinard and Lasker. At the time (I believe) Adrian was placed at free safety while I played strong. I recall the running play to my side, the boundary side, and my responsibility was to force the play inside towards the linebackers. Jeff Rutledge hiked the ball and pitched it to the running back—I can't remember whom it was at the time and I also couldn't see. I couldn't see him because although I walked by these players every day, this was the first time I saw linemen running towards me, and they were huge! I believe it was Brad Benson; he was big and could run. He ran so well as he came up with his outstretched arms and blocked me twenty yards down field! His outstretched locked arms shut down every attempt I made to get around him. I didn't make that tackle, and I know Coach Belichick noticed along with Romeo what happened on the play and would be watching me closely after that debacle. I would have to redeem myself during these drills because time was running out even though we were only three days into camp. Couple plays in which I made assisted tackles in, I heard Belichick make general statements about the defense doing well. That's good, but it did nothing for me individually to be noticed. I had to do something during this period. The opportunity presented itself when I was lined up in the boundary again, and something came to me to be ready and that possibly the offense and those big lineman were coming my way again. This time I was ready. "Hike," as the quarterback made the call. It was a sweep again, and this time OJ Anderson was carrying the ball. OJ had already solidified himself as a great running back with St. Louis Cardinals and as a member of the 1986 Super Bowl team and future Hall of Famer. OJ is six foot two, two hundred and twenty pounds, a strong and fast running back that was heading my way on a sweep. I was ready this time, and I knew a big lineman was coming around the corner ready to drive me down field again. This time I was ready though and this time I came up fast and got behind the line of scrimmage before the lineman could square his shoulders and a prepare to hit the first face he sees. I got low behind the oncoming lineman as OJ attempted to cut it up into the line of scrimmage. I was able to squeeze down into the hole and hit him low on his thighs and held on tight until help from the rest of the defense came along. I was elated that I was able to make one solo play on the day, but I felt bad (pain) because of OJ's thighs. His thighs were like tree trunks, and when I ran into them, it felt like I hit the entire tree. I got up off the shredded grass field and shook my head to clear my thoughts shook up a bit, not too shook up to leave the field but enough t as I left the pile, and headed back to the huddle to gather my senses. For the rest of the practice it went like that, hard running, hard hitting and bodies leaving the field after crushing hits between offense and defensive players. I made it out of the day in one piece as one of the fortunate rookies without an injury and ready to get back at it on another day. As we all came together at the end of practice and broke down in he middle of the field at the end of practice, I looked to the sidelines and looked at all the fans waiting for us to leave the field again. The feeling of being a professional athlete is something I can't explain or describe in detail. To see children and adults waiting to see your name on a piece of paper, shake your hand, or just hear you say hello to them leaves a feeling of responsibility to your community knowing you feel bigger than you think you are in the eyes of others and actions affect many others if you know them or not. That's the good, but there is also a false sense of grandeur that gives athletes a false sense of invincibility, which in itself is dangerous. I believe many (not all) professional athletes have this feeling about themselves after reaching such heights on the gridiron or parquet floors. I believe we all have seen it played out on television by today's athletes more than ever before. The praise of fans towards players brings a sense of high importance in a society that thrives on sports and entertainment. I'll be honest, I felt a little more important walking of the field after practice that day and even more elevated when I heard a familiar voice call my name "Yo, Pat!" The call wasn't like a fan calling; it was more like someone that new me personally, and it was. It was Reggie Plair. Reggie was from Brooklyn, NY and was my back up at Southern. Reggie was my height at six foot three, and although I played at Southern at 185, Reggie was bigger at 195 and could hit and run. Reggie reminded me of myself when trying to remember the coverages and making the right calls my freshman year however. Reggie was now going into his junior year and would be the starting free safety at Southern. "What you doing here, Reggie?"

"I came to see you," he said. I felt humbled and flattered he would travel to Pleasantville, NY to see me. I asked him if he enjoyed the practice. He said yes and that "my back peddle looked good out there." He said, "You look good out there and you can hang with these guys." Well, an endorsement like that adds to the confidence and encouragement a rookie player needs when moving forward. I stood there; young kids came running up asking for my autograph, which I obliged. As I became overwhelmed with the kids and adults, Reggie said he'd catch up with me later and "keep doing your thing, Pat." By the time I looked up, Reggie was gone and before I could tell him thanks.

Going into the second week of camp, I felt good but still not sure where I stood on the debt chart. By now I had ten practices under my belt, and I felt better about picking up my responsibilities at strong safety. I recognize Adrian was no longer in my team group and the only comfortable face was Haddix who I saw nightly before I laid my head down for the night. I still had a sense of apprehension heading into Monday's practice. Monday was a bright and sunny day. I remember putting my equipment on and Adrian saying to me, "Let's go today." He was encouraging and saw that I would get in the " mix" with him on and off the field. If there was nothing else, I did get in the "mix." I was not afraid and I was not afraid to hit you. Adrian respected that from a small school guy like me, and he really didn't care what school you came from, as long as you came to play and play hard. Well Monday was a good day. Monday morning practice like usual consisted of walk through and review. It was the afternoon practices that I was most anxious about and couldn't wait to get to. The defense was shuffled around this Monday afternoon practice, and I was placed at free safety and Adrian was moved to strong safety. I was surprised by the change, but I wasn't complaining because now I was at a position that I felt comfortable playing. At free safety, I was one of the best. I was able to cover the field with my range from hash mark to hash mark, and my understanding of routes run by the receivers was A +. At strong safety you don't see the entire field so you don't get a true sense of what's going on around you in the backfield. So being back at free safety put me in a mentally different mindset of confidence and intensity knowing that anyone coming in my area would reap the reward of a thorough Pat Morrison hit! One of the plays coming my way was a "play action" by Phil Simms and a throw back to Bavaro running up the seam. I saw it coming and made a break on the ball running directly to Bavaro. I didn't totally lose my mind and forget my status as a rookie and his as a veteran. I was a rookie, and the worst thing a rookie could do is hurt an all-pro, multi-millionaire championship tight end. So as I took off in his direction and closed in on him, I yelled out letting know I was there as the ball was just about reached him, which forced him to react to me thinking this rookie wasn't thinking, which caused him to focus on me, which caused him to miss the ball, and in frustration he shoved me. His shove threw me off line, but I didn't go down and he didn't catch the ball. A couple plays down came a running play. It was a right off of tackle running play to Joe Morris. Joe stood five foot eight about 200 pounds who played running back out of Syracuse, NY. As the played developed again, I could see and I recognized the play. As I ran towards the line through the alley way (like I was taught at Southern), I saw Joe get he ball heading my way. Adrian saw it too as we both moved in towards Joe, as we both collided into Joe at the same time knocking him back and down in a hurry. I know I got a good shot in on him square up and it was confirmed by Adrian when he got up and said, "Damn boy, that's way to come up and lay it on him."

Joe looked around, got up, and said, "Who was that who hit me like that? Good hit, rookie," as he headed back to the offensive huddle. Today I was noticed for doing what I'm known for. I was known for coming up and stopping the run and laying people out. But even after that moment, I didn't feel I was being positioned in the right spot for my abilities and talents. Practice went on for a few more plays and it then abruptly ended. "I was just getting started," I thought to myself. Tomorrow is another day, and hopefully I'll gets another chance at Free Safety.

As usual as the team left the field, we would be bombarded my autograph seekers, young and old, looking to get a lifetime memory to show their friends at school or put in their sports rooms back home. There were not only children along the chained fence line but also young women, alone quietly standing by waiting for a hello from the players as they walked by. I noticed this as I made my way through the gates and observed how causally these women made themselves known and that they were there to meet them as well as to let certain players know that "I'm here waiting for you." It was an interesting dynamic at work. Growing up, you heard the stories for Joe Namath, Joe DiMaggio, Mickey Mantle, Wilt Chamberlain, and even my childhood English superstar "football" player in England George Best and the choices of women they had available for "companionship" If they wanted. And now I could see it in full operation mode, and it was exciting and revealing to a young twenty-two-year-old still finding his way through American culture. As I made my way past the gates and headed towards the locker room, I noticed a group of women behind a table giving out lunch boxes to children who appeared to be at Pace University for summer camp or some other activity. As I strolled closer, I recognized someone, and I looked twice because I couldn't believe what I was seeing. It was my mother! She was giving out lunches to the children at the camp. "Mom, what you doing here?" (It was obvious) "You didn't tell me."

She said, "Hi, son," with a smile and went on to say she didn't know she was coming there until a few days earlier and continued with her work. Well it was good to see her because it was going on two weeks since I last saw her, but I also felt weird to see her in front of my teammates giving out lunches. I was ashamed of my mother's struggle to provide, which I felt was vulnerable to social American criticism. She asked me how I was doing. I said good, and like most mothers she asked me, "Have you been eating? You look skinny." She was right, and although I was eating all I could at lunch and dinner, I still lost a few pounds. I was down to 189-190, down 4 pounds from 194. One thing I didn't need was to lose weight. I needed to gain or the very least maintain.

"Yes, Mom, I've been eating." I kept moving after that because I didn't want to bring too much attention to myself and my mother working giving out lunches. Before I left, however, she introduced me to her coworker who requested an autograph and commended Mom on having a football Giants son. By the afternoon practice, Mom was gone for the day, and we were back "at it" reviewing and drilling all that we had learned that morning.

By Wednesday of the second week, the team was jelling much better, as you witnessed players flying around and making big hits on the rookie offensive players and watching the veterans and top drafted receivers making great catches against rookie defenders. I still could not figure out how Stephen Baker could make so many great catches in the middle hounds looking to crush anything that came across its defense. He was a fearless receiver who would go over the middle if he were asked to do so, as well as make those unbelievable catches down the field as we all witnessed in the 1990 Super Bowl. It was quite evident how he obtained his well-deserved nickname "Touchdown Maker." Mark Ingram from the first day was just smooth and effortless with his route running. You could see why he and the others attended big time schools and why they were drafted where they were. Things were going well, and Coach Parcells reminded us in a few weeks that we would be having our first pre-season game against the New England Patriots. I was excited about that, but I wasn't sure if I would be around for that game. I was excited because "California boy" Rick Atkinson had signed with New England and I heard he was doing well. It would be good to see him, but only time would tell, with opportunity and luck.

That night after dinner and the usual meetings and before I started reviewing my playbook, I decided to make some calls home to give Mom and Kandice an update. Mom asked the usual questions, if I'm eating enough and " if I feel confident." I told her yes and I would have told her yeahs even if I wasn't. I wouldn't want to worry her while I was away. Also I did feel a little pressure to do well with the hopes of getting us out of the run-down Platzner apartment building we lived in. When I think of it, I remember for months our apartment smelled terrible, and no matter how much we cleaned the house with Clorox, air fresheners, and Arm and Hammer, the rank smell always remained.

We called "the supa" up couple of times to rid the smell, and it got worst as weeks passed by, but he didn't appear to be too concerned. One day, he finally came up and spent some time as we all searched to determine where the rank, dead smell was coming from. We pinpointed a spot by the couch in the living room. We picked up the sofa anxiously hoping to find something, but nothing was there to see. The smell however was even stronger. We followed the smell right to the couch again. " It must be here," supa said. He cut open the side of the fabric woven couch, and the stench came rushing out. He opened it more, and he saw something inside as he put his gloves on as I stepped back and away from him and the couch. It was giant city RAT! It had died in the couch and was decomposing in it. It was things like this along with no lights in the basement where the trash would have to be delivered and no lights in the hallways sometimes. I remember as a child I was initially scared to bring the trash down there from the fifth floor to the basement, throw it in the area of the big trash collectors, and quickly turn around and run back upstairs or out into the courtyard, yards away through he dark, dingy, rat-invested basement. Mom would always say "can't wait to get out Platzner building." That is and still is the owner of the building on North Ave.

"All is well, Mom, and wish me luck," I said.

" Good luck, son, okay goodnight."

I called Kandice next and told her about my day and that I felt good. She congratulated me and wished me lots of luck and encouraged me to keep working hard no matter what. After a couple of minutes of small talk about her cousins and West Hills, Kandice said she had something to tell me. My internal antennas went up and I wondered what she had to say that couldn't have been said as part of our ongoing conversation that it had its own section to focus in on? With a low voice she said she was PRE-GANAT! I couldn't believe what I was hearing. I just turned twenty-two years old, just graduated from college, and was about to begin my life either on the football field, back to school to get a master's degree, or get a job in corporate America, but a baby was not in my immediate plans, and the way our relationship was at the time, the future was not solidified. I said, "How far are you?" and she said, "three months." That put the timeframe when I was staying at her parent's house preparing for camp. I asked her, "Weren't you on the Pill?" And she said she was but stopped because it was affecting her body, so she stopped. I said, "What you going to do?"

She said, "I'm having the baby, and I hope you'll be there to support her and my child." Well I knew very well how it feels not to have a father in the home and I never wanted any of that for my children, not to have me with them or at least know I'm in there life. I said "okay, we'll talk later" and hung up the phone. I didn't sleep well that night, and I didn't feel like studying either. The conversation took me for a turn emotionally and mentally. I didn't know what the future would hold for me; I didn't know if I could or knew how to be a father, and I didn't know if I could support the baby and her mother. Football was now secondary in my head, and I knew I had to make this work. As much as I wanted to, I also knew that although I had a great day at practice, it wouldn't be enough to prolong my time and make the team, because the decision wasn't mine to make; it was in the hands of God and Coach Parcells. But if for nothing else, if I were to make the team, and if nothing else would come about with Kandice and me, at least knew I could take care of the baby financially. I told Haddix about my call, and his response was more of a "wow" and "it will be okay." His was response wasn't too consoling or comforting for me, and I felt my anger reemerge with an overwhelming feeling of grief and desperation.

CHAPTER FOUR
A NEW GAME

The game of life is unpredictable, with its twist and turns, not knowing what awaits you around the next corner. So it was with me and Kandice and my current situation in Pleasantville, NY. I didn't sleep well that night, and although Thursday morning was bright and sunny, there was an air of glume and depression that left a level of fright in my soul. I went out that day, and I found myself one step behind when covering the receivers. I covered Stacy Robinson on one play, and I found myself so far out of position that I just gave up on the play. I've never given up on a play in my life, but that morning practice would go down as one of my worst practices while wearing a football uniform. Having a practice like that at this most crucial moment in camp was the worst thing that could happen to me. At this point of camp, players are being evaluated and critiqued with a more critical eye, drawing closer to have to make those decisions based on what they see today and not what tomorrow may or may not bring. At this point in camp, every series and every down counts toward a player's longevity in the league, and having a morning like that wasn't comforting but more like a strike against me. I made it through practice that Thursday morning, and as I was walking off the field, Coach Romeo ran up to me and asked me if everything was okay. I didn't want to tell him the latest news and how it left me mentally and emotionally unstable, plus I didn't want to use it as an excuse for my poor play. As a professional athlete, especially in the NFL, there are young men lined up wishing and hoping for and opportunity like the one I had and don't have the concerns that I have and are free to play and willing to do what ever they can to play in the National Football League. So if I complained, it only would fall on deaf ears anyway. I told him, "All is well, Coach" and "I'll have a better practice this afternoon." At lunch, I sat a table where most of he DBs sat, listening to the jokes and laughter of Kinard, Collins, and "Toast." I couldn't find myself to laugh at any of it because my mind was elsewhere wandering about the baby on the way. The fragility of the relationship between Kandice and me wore heavy on me, and I was scared not knowing what my mother would say. At 22, I felt I was done. I felt that everything I had worked for up to this point was falling apart and my future was doomed. I finished my lasagna and cranberry juice and headed to the locker room to rest up for the afternoon practice. As I sat at my locker and waited for practice to begin, I decided to call Kandice back and ask her if she was sure that she was pregnant and was she sure she was going to keep the baby. In my distraught moment, I was hoping to hear from her lips a different answer and I was anxious to find a solution that would put my mind at ease. Nothing came to mind, but what did come to mind was Aunt Louise hitting me upside my head and pinching me on my side and the rank smell of urine in my nose. These reflections and moments in my life caused me much pain, and I was in a negative and hopeless moment of psycho-emotional state on this day, looking for a way to ease the pain. She said, "Yes, I'm pregnant, and I'm having it with or without you!" She could sense my anxiety and questioning "options" to satisfy my ignorance, but there was no conceding by her. She was pregnant, and I was going to be a father, with or without football, so I better be ready. The afternoon practice went a little better. I played with a sense of urgency and aggression. However, that combination without a cognitive balance is a recipe for disaster. There are many great athletes *not* playing professional sports today, not because they don't have the necessary skills, talent or ability, but possibly because they're missing the mental and emotional fortitude piece of the game. I've seen many basketball players in high school and in college, on organized teams or pickup games, that could shoot anywhere on the court or take off from the foul line and duck it. But unfortunately if they only had a better grasp and understanding of the mental restraint and will to take on the task of excellence, then possibly none of you reading this book would know of my journey, because easily my position at Southern would have been taken from one of these great athletes. But things work for the goodness of the lord, so if having a baby is the lord's plan, then I must play my best with the hand I was dealt. These men that I'm talking about for some reason didn't have the drive or mental capacity to be coached or wanted to be in a competitive environment to be gazed upon and critiqued for the good and bad. All they wanted to do was play for the love of the game and not for money or fame. At this point I wasn't sure what I wanted anymore. I definitely loved the game that I fell in love with since that first time in 1975. But the mental pressure was heavier than any three hundred pound offensive tackle coming around the end, and it felt like I was being driven down life's secondary path, and I couldn't get out of the way. I practiced hard and ran faster with a sense of urgency as another day drew to an end in the life of a rookie in the NFL. We had meetings later that night with our position coaches and team, the entire team defense. As the film rolled along capturing the day's practice events, it was refreshing to see myself on the big screen throughout drills. The disappointing part was that I wasn't making enough plays on the one-on-ones during our skeleton drills against the receivers. I was one step behind. The ball would reach the receivers hands, and then I would just miss knocking it away or not be there to make the tackle. The NFL wants play-makers who can turn the ball over and give the offense more chances to score. Me not being in position to make that happen more frequently than others who demonstrated they could put me at an disadvantage moving forward for the coaches' evaluation. During team time, I did much better, and Belichick mentioned how we were all coming along. He pointed out at moments during film that the lack of effort by veterans and rookies by calling out Elvis Patterson (Toast) for his lack of effort getting to the ball, as well as missed plays. If you weren't being consistent with "your job" expectations, Belecheck had very few words for you, and if he told you once or twice, he expected you to get it the third time and execute it as expected, and if not, it would be time to move on to the next person who could. I was somewhere in the middle. Doing well sometimes and inconsistent at other times. Walking back to my room, my head started wondering again into the unknown. I started thinking about what would I do if I don't make the team? My mind was scrambled again, and I just couldn't get to my room fast enough to go to sleep. Haddix was already in bed with his playbook in hand studying. I walked in, sat on my bed, and opened my playbook and began to review what Coach Belichick was emphasizing in position meeting. It's been but a few minutes later when Coach Sweatman knocked on the door and said, "Lights out."

Friday morning practice was spent on special teams. It appeared as time drew closer to the beginning of the season, more time was spent on fine-tuning the offense, defense, and special teams, as well as fine-tuning the second and third team players. Most of the starters new they would be back the coming season, but there were a few that were on the fringes. I just wanted to do my best with the hopes of having a spot. There was another DB who the year before played a couple of games for the Miami Dolphins in 1986. D. Brown we called him, who played corner, and he had experience in the league. I knew he would be given a good look going into the third week. Friday afternoon practice went well. I made plays by knocking the ball down a few times and just being in position in other situations. I felt good, and my attitude changed for the better. I couldn't be discouraged and go on thinking about what might be, and deal with what is. I had to go out and play my best and hope it wasn't too late to prove my worth. Romeo said I had a better practice in the afternoon and that I should keep it up. "Yes, Coach," I said. It's always a good thing when a coach speaks to a player; it provides a sense of comfort and tension release knowing they are pleasing their coach. Because when a coach doesn't speak to his player, that's when you worry, and that's when something is about to happen and not necessarily in the player's favor.

Saturday was scheduled as an inter-squad scrimmage with referees. I would have an opportunity to play unrestricted and hopefully demonstrate I can play with my peers. I was taped up, buckled up ready to go, and I felt good. I was ready to take on the offense of Simms, OJ, Joe, Crocihiccia, and the Touchdown Maker. The first offense was up going against the second defense. I would be starting at the free safety position, and Adrian would be at the strong safety position. Wayne Haddix was at one corner and D. Brown at another. We were about to get it in. It was a hard-hitting first series of plays with big runs against our defense because once the running backs got into the secondary, the DBs couldn't deliver a full hit on the runner. Our second team defense front line couldn't hold up against the 1986 Super Bowl Giants Championship offensive line. Our secondary didn't do much better. The timing plays were on point. We were missing plays on the short patterns. You saw the greatness of Simms, Manuel, Mowatt, Ingram, and Baker who had made their way into the starting rotation for the scrimmage as they made their way down the field on our making catches on our defense. After the first series, I was put in again towards the end of the scrimmage where I came up and made a good tackle on Lee Rouson. Adrian once again congratulated me on coming up. But two plays later my opportunities ended; the scrimmage was over, and practice had come to an end for the day. We all came to the middle of the field being called up by Johnny Parker as the other assistant coaches made their way off the field, headed back to the field house. Parcells broke us down, but he first told us that he saw some good things and some things that needed to happen and improve from the young players if they wanted to make the team. He reinforced that playing in the NFL was a privilege and a great job to have. He stated that there are *not* too many professions that allow you to play a game and get paid a lot of money. I said in my head, "I want this job and I want that money too," because a lot depended on it. Coach broke us down for the rest of the day and we all headed back to the locker rooms. On the way out of the practice gate area, as usual, the children and fans were looking for autographs as they bombarded and my teammates and me again. I did my best to give as may autographs out as I could, because I recognized this would be a once in a lifetime opportunity to live the life of a professional athlete, and at the same time have so many people appreciating you for the job you do and the joy you bring to their lives. I stayed and gave as many autographs as I could before making my way back to the locker room. I noticed that not too many veterans were giving out autographs as they left that up to the rookies. I believe they understood that there's a long season ahead of them and they would be signing a lot of autographs throughout the sixteen-game season.

For the first time during camp, we were given the Sunday off to rest. That was a blessing because we were going non-stop for the past three weeks, getting up early, having a full day of practices, early meetings, late meetings, and late bedtimes. Having the day off felt like heaven. I didn't have a car at the time so I couldn't go home for the day to see Mom, so I just sat around, studied the playbook, and hung out with the rest of the players in the dorm area. For a moment I had stopped thinking of my future with Kandice and the new baby on the way and just relaxed and took in the moment as a professional football player. The life isn't easy as I got to see up close and personal. Players have the same concerns and life problems as me and everyone else in the world. Guys are on the phones talking to wives and girlfriends getting off the phones in the hallways angry and happy. There was a spectrum of emotions, animation, and laughter throughout the dorm area on Sunday morning. As the new week approached, I knew there would be another round of cuts to be handed out. I wasn't sure if I had made it to the sixty-man roster yet, and I would not know until the knock on the door came this night or sometime during the following week. I went to bed soundly Sunday night, saying my prayers and giving thanks to God for providing the opportunity to be in Pleasantville, NY and to be playing football. Haddix had said his prayers after me, and we both went to bed wondering what tomorrow would bring. Well Sunday night I didn't get a knock on my door by Sweatman so I rested easy that night and thought about what I needed to do on the field on Monday. The jitters and anxiety were gone, and I felt ready to go out and perform the way I knew how to and give my best.

Monday was here, and I was ready to go. I made it over to the cafeteria and had some cranberry juice, eggs, and bacon then headed over to the locker room where the fans were out as usual awaiting our arrival. I found it amazing that fans would be up so early at the field site even before we got there. I did rookie professional duty which was to sign a few autographs before I reached the field and before my day begun. Today, I pulled out my Nike three-quarter cleats. I had only worn them once since I've been in camp and was saving them for later. Later was now, and I felt good in Nike because that's what I wore at Southern Connecticut, and I performed well in them. I got a new pair of blue gloves for my hands, and after getting my ankles taped up, I headed out with Adrian to the field. Coach Parcells brought us up to the middle of the field and told us some players were let go over the weekend and a few more will be unfortunately being let go this week too. We all (rookies) knew our time was limited and we just needed to do our best and hopefully we'll make the 45-man roster. In the Common Era, the roster size is 53 including eight "inactive" players who teams call "practice players," totaling sixty-one (61). These players can move up any time during the season and become "active players" and be counted towards their active time in the NFL. Basically, a player can be a "member" of a team and be "inactive" the entire season and his time counted in the NFL is *zero*! Truth be told, with my new situation, I didn't care if I was active or inactive; I needed the money for my new baby and my new life. Coach told us to keep working hard, and he even pointed out some veterans that needed to get their act together or they'll be out of Pleasantville too. As we broke down into our groups, I said hello to Coach Romeo like I usually do, but he didn't respond back as he usually does with a few words of encouragement. At the time, I didn't think anything of it and kept on to my group. Coach Fontes and Sweatman put us through our paces and drills as we prepared for one-on-ones again with the receivers, then against first O in team. My one-on-one coverage was tighter than it was from the beginning of camp. I went up against Phil McConkey, former Navy player and who caught a touchdown in the Super Bowl. Phil was short, about 5'8, but quick. But after a few days working and running with the recent top draft picks, I knew I could cover him. He came up fast on me, but the way he was running, I recognized that he was trying to push me down field so he could stop and break in or out on me. I was ready. He pushed down field, but I settled down and caught him in my grasp, as he stopped and attempted to break out towards the sidelines. I was on him! I cut in front of him waiting for the ball to come my way and for my first interception. It didn't happen because the ball was thrown badly, low and behind both of us. "Shit!" I said to myself as I picked up the ball and tossed it to Phil, as he ran back to the huddle. The "team" portion of practice was coming up in a few minutes. The stations got shorter as the days grew closer to pre-season. The Giants had to get the team down to fifty-five (55) by the first season game so time was up with detailed teaching. Time was at hand to make an impact, make plays, and stand out. The defense was called out this time by Coach Belichick. He called out the defensive line first, then the linebackers, then lastly the DBs. Haddix got called—he was a corner—D. Brown, the other corner; next was Adrian at strong safety then a veteran Greg Lasker at free safety. I wasn't called out to the second defensive backfield like I had always. I didn't know what to think because I hadn't been in this situation before and I had a few days of good play and always worked hard. I looked at it as that the coaches wanted to evaluate more and look at different defensive backfields. The rest of us sat back and watched. Me and Lovelady, a receiver from University of Memphis, who the year previously was with the Redskins, made the roster for a few games before he was released. He was small at 5'8 but ran good patterns, good hands with decent speed. Next to him was a lineman from Nebraska. A huge man, 6'5, 300 pounds but was soft. I remember him because he was picked above me in the 10th round where I was told later they were looking for me at that point. We all stood there watching, as the defense was out on the field and the players giving there all. After going back and forth between the first team offense against the second team defense and the first team defense against the second team offense, I was called out to replace Lasker and put back to free safety. With me being at free safety, I knew I would be able give my all and play free freely because I was comfortable playing at my "home position" and I was ready show them what I could do.

The first play was a running play, and I came up as quickly as I could, but the runner was tackled. I was ready and excited and no more anxiety. The next play was a throw to the sidelines and completed to Lovelady. We broke the huddle for the next play when all of a sudden the whistle was blown by Johnny Parker signaling practice was over. " What!" I said to myself. "I just got in." Something came over me like a dark shadow of gloom. I wasn't sure what it initially was, but I new it wasn't good. My best mental and emotional day came to an end just like that, and there were no more time or opportunities to show and prove today. The usual end of practice comments were made by Coach Parcells and Parker as we were broken down to head to dinner and back to the dorms. As I walked off the field, I actually didn't feel like signing autographs and only signed two or three, ducked behind some other players, and ran to the locker room. Eating dinner with Lovelady, Odessa, Baker, and a few other players just listening to their stories of being in other camps and playing at the schools they had just left a few months earlier had me thinking about all these young men looking to further their lives and depending on making the league to change their family's current economic status. Some of them could have been in the same situation as myself, have something or someone depending on them to make the team. It felt like a cattle call with only a few would be selected as the best to breed or in this case to make the 50-man roster. After dinner, I went to my room to relax on my bed and think. I thought about everything the day I had brought, Kandice and the soon to come baby, my mom, Raymond, Southern—everything ran through my head that evening. Haddix hadn't come back directly to the room after dinner. I didn't feel like studying the playbook this night, so I looked over a couple of pages and then went to bed. I didn't hear Haddix come in, but sometime between 9:30 and 10:00 o'clock he came in. It must have been two hours later around midnight when I heard the door knock. I got up to answer it, and when I opened it is when I saw Coach Sweatman. He looked at me and said, "Coach Parcells wants to see you before practice." Pause. "And bring your playbook." He turned away and walked away. Before I could settle back into my sleep and could hear more knocks down the dormitory hallway as Sweatman was passing along the dreaded news. Although he didn't say it, I knew that was the knock that said your time was up with the Giants.

The morning came, and I went to breakfast for a quick bite (last bite) and headed over to the field house locker room to meet with Coach Parcells. There were other players waiting to meet with him too. I was next up, and the meeting was short and quick as to what Coach had to say. It would be interesting to hear what he had to say about me on this day. I entered the office and Coach Parcells was sitting behind his desk as he greeted me with a handshake. He said, "Take a seat." I took a seat as he informed me that the Giants were letting me go. He said I would be put on waivers for two weeks for other NFL teams to have the opportunity to pick me up and another opportunity to finish out the summer. I wanted to say that I knew it took awhile for me to come around, but I've started to get it, the flow, the speed, the intensity and everything, but I knew it would do no good. He said that initially it appeared that magnitude of playing in front of big crowds might too much for me, but then he realized over the past week that it wasn't the case because "I saw you coming around and made good strides." Unfortunately my time had run out to show and prove that I was capable of playing in the NFL. Sometimes during life's journey, as endless as it may seem at the moment, time *will* run out, and so there must be a sense of urgency in our actions, urgency in execution and delivery because you may not get a second chance, and all things have their appointed time. I didn't get a second chance and my time was up and I had to head back up the road to New Ro. Coach wished me good luck and wished me the best on my journey. I thanked him and headed out of he office and into the locker room. Adrian's locker was next to mine, and I told him that I got released. He had a surprised and disappointed look on his face. I told him it was my pleasure to meet and play with him and hoped we could stay in touch. I went over to Odessa and Lovelady and told them too. They were surprised too that I was let go but said, "You'll get picked up of waivers because you can play." I went back to locker to clean it out, but I realized my pads were already gone along with my helmet. I was planning on taking my Nike and Adidas cleats with me, but in the moment of disappearing and disappointment I didn't. I was depressed, upset, disappointed, and embarrassed. Was it true what one of my teammates said: "I wasn't good enough"? Was it true when my mom said "are you confident"? I don't know what the reason was, maybe all of the above or not of it at all. It could be just the nature of professional sports where there are just a few spots for so many. I packed my bag in the locker room with the little toiletries I had, some socks, shirts, and shorts, and left to return to the dorm to pack the rest of my things. I was emotionally drained and mentally down, but more in shock and wasn't actually sure what my next steps would be. Would I just sit at home for he next week or so and see if I was going to be picked up of waivers? As I waited from the field house wondering how I would get home, Jim Crocicchia, the quarterback from the University of Penn came up to me and asked me if I needed a ride. He was let go too and was heading home to his home in Westchester close to New Ro. He offered me a ride, and I sad sure, and within fifteen minutes we were off in his Red BMW 325 convertible with the top down heading down the hutch towards home.

CHAPTER FIVE
TO ENDURE

"Later, Cro," I said as Crocichicca pulled off and got on the 95. I ran up stairs with my bags in hand and opened apartment 12B on the 5th floor, threw my bags down, and cried. Anguish came over me as I laid there in our rat-infested apartment. All I could think about was where I had just came from, just 26 miles away from beautiful suburban Pleasantville, NY with high hopes, dreams, and the possibilities of changing my living conditions and a home with grass and maybe a pool, to my reality of an apartment dwelling, operated by a negligent landlord, above a shoe shine store, consignment shop, and an Army recruiting station. After a couple of minutes of feeling sorry for myself, I got up and went look to see if anyone else was home. The house was quiet as I made my way to the kitchen to find something to eat. Like most times there was something on the stove or in the refrigerator from the previous night that Dad or my mother cooked. And like always, there sat in the heavy black skillet was a mixed masterpiece of brown dirty rice, carrots, chopped chicken, colorful peppers, spices, and greens sitting in a base of sauce from the magic of mixers of the Caribbean homeland. After I ate my full plate, I called Icky. I told him what happened and that I was home. I asked him what he was doing and he said he "just got home so come over." My friend greeted me like he always did since 4th grade with a "pound" and a hug. He said, "Don't worry about that shit; you'll get picked up. If not you'll be working like the rest of us." That was true, but I didn't want just any job. I wanted a career. I wanted a career in the National Football League. I did have my degree in Corporate Communications and Media, so I thought I could always go back up to New Britain, Connecticut and apply for a position at ESPN. I remember my advisor told me about this young developing sports channel in New Britain, Connecticut and that I would do good there behind the mic. This journey however wasn't over for me yet in my mind, so getting a "job" at ESPN or anywhere else wasn't in my immediate plans. Icky and I hung out in his living room while his parents were out and watched some sports on ESPN and Speed Racer cartoons. I returned home later that evening to find Mom home. She noticed my bags in my room, so when she heard the door open she called out to me "Pat, you home?"

"Yes, Ma, I'll be right there," I said as I made my way slowly to her room. I explained the best I could about how I thought I practiced, the limited numbers, and waiver system, but I wasn't sure she fully understood everything or anything I said because she said, "Maybe if you were more confident the coach may have seen that and kept you." I always felt slighted when she would say that about confidence, and for the first time it really hit me that I may have been playing too conscious and that may have come across as hesitant or not sure of myself. There maybe a little bit of both in trying not to make mistakes and be perfect, and in doing so not allowing the Giants to see my full ability to perform every down every day at a high level that they expect from a player at the NFL level. When I finally got it together in the last week, my time had run out and I was sent home. I told Mom that I felt confident but I probably could have done some things differently. I called my agent Rich Glickel in Spring Valley, NY and gave him the update on what happened. He said we'd see what happens with waivers and go from there. Rich was not a full-time agent and attorney who provided legal and contractual counseling for me who was recommended to me by Kerry Taylor, my former teammate from Southern who eventually went to the CFL and played a couple of years up there. Kerry trusted him and I trusted Kerry, and so I trusted him and his advice. When I told him what happened, he offered his continued support and representation if I was claimed off waivers. But what I liked most about Rich was that he had a good sense of my situation and the financial end to my employment with the Giants and didn't request any compensation for his time or services rendered earlier. As we spoke more about football, he offered me opportunities to go to Canada and play there. At the time I knew very little about Canadian football, its salaries, or its influence in the football world. I looked at his proposal to go to the CFL as a minor league opportunity of American football, instead of another real football league and another real opportunity. I told Rich no because I wanted to play in the NFL and that I would wait on waivers and take my chances there on getting picked up. After I hung up with Rich, I had to inform mom of my situation with Kandice and the baby on the way. After I hung up the sky blue rotatory phone in the kitchen, I went back into Mom's room to tell her the news. My brother

Michael was in his room playing with his gadgets under the fort he built in his room. I sat down on the end of her bed as she rested watching TV and dreaded the thought of telling her the news. I got up the nerve and told her that Kandice was pregnant and that I was going to be a father. She was shocked by this news and momentarily looked at me without saying anything. I dropped my head in shame, believing I disappointed her and was letting down. She must have seen my discontent and sadness and wanted to know how long Kandice was pregnant, and what I was going to do next. I told her what Kandice had told me and that I would be there for her. Mom did say, "You're just getting your life started and now you have bills before you get started." (Kissing her teeth.)

"I know, Ma, I know," I said. She saw the disappointment on my face, so she didn't push more on the subject. It was a trying time and a heavy load knowing that I now had this responsibility after getting released from the only job I had up to this point. I went back to my room to lie back down and fell asleep listening to 107.5 WBLS FM.

The next day, Wednesday, I got up and called Kandice and told her the news of my release. She was empathic and expressed her concerns and wanted to know what was next. I told her about the waiver process and that I would be waiting at home in New Rochelle if I got a call from a team, and if need be, I would be ready to travel somewhere right away. I would be staying in New Rochelle and training to stay prepared if the call would come. I tried to stay optimistic over the phone, but I also knew that all the teams were making mandated cuts to get down to 50 players by opening day. Now that I was home, I was anxious to see the first pre-season game coming up this Sunday. "California boy" Rick Atkinson, my teammate, had signed with the New England Patriots as a cornerback, after coming off an All-American season and Walter Camp inductee. Rick was the example of not having all the "numbers" as preferred in the NFL like weight and speed, but what he did posses was an high IQ for the game and he studied it daily. For his efforts and time put in at Southern, he too signed an immediate free agent contract and was ready to show the NFL another Southern guy who came out to join me and Matt Mclees who went to the Cleveland Browns and of course Scott who had been drafted in the fifth round by the San Diego Chargers. I told myself I would stay low in New Ro until after the game because those who may not have read the papers that week wouldn't hace known I was released until after watching the Sunday game, which then they would have and noticed by then that I wasn't on the field. Sunday arrived, and I didn't feel like going to church with mom, so I told her I would go next week if that was alright with her. Church was a very important part in my life and not going with her this Sunday morning disappointed her again. Honestly, I was still embarrassed about being released right before the first preseason game. I shouldn't have however because the congregation of "island people" who really didn't know much about American football and the processes or protocols couldn't have cared less if I made the team or not. All the church family would have wanted to know was if I was well, if was still "saved by the blood of Jesus" and that they missed me in church. The church family of my New Rochelle congregation of the Pentecostal denomination was and is my support and comfort place. The members that remain to this day and those that have passed along to "glory" have been the ones who have supported me and kept me in their prayers for the past four years in college and being out in the world. I no longer wonder why I'm still here. It's because of God's grace, mercy, and the prayers of the church members of the Church of God of Prophesy in New Rochelle. My experience growing up in that fold is different from the one I experienced with Aunt Louise in England years earlier.

When I finally got out of bed late Sunday morning, I thought I would clean up my room a bit. Although my trash can wasn't too far from my bed, I realized I left a glass of juice on the floor and next to the juice was an empty chocolate Kit Kat wrapper. Dad had come home late Saturday night and bought it for me. He and Mom were drifting apart more and more which forced him to move out and rent a room in a house not to far away on a street called Sickles Avenue. He was always welcomed in our home, but when he had drinking episodes, he was not allowed in. He scared us sometimes, and my brother was still small in elementary school, impressionable, and consequently Mom didn't want any of us exposed to his frequent drunken ways. It was the plight of two polar systems pulling on each other. Because when he wasn't drinking, he was the kindest, funniest, smartest, most intelligent man who I had met up to that time, and who read and wrote everything down about his thoughts on the subject. His sarcasm was welcomed too. I knew he wanted me to question myself of my accomplishments and to question who I was competing against to measure my success. Even in his drunken moments he had some good lessons and he would say, "I may not be your biological, but I'm still your father, boy." Him being home, I knew there was something cooking in the kitchen, and all I heard were dishes and the sizzling sounds of grease popping, and the aroma of onions and whatever else added spices he added to his gourmet creation. I got up quickly and picked up off the floor my night before snack and tossed it in the trash and headed to the shower. After my shower and Vaseline lotion up after, I went into the kitchen where I found Dad sitting quietly reading the Sunday newspaper. I told him what happened, but he didn't say much and I could see on his face that he wasn't sure what to say. I told him about the process and hopefully I would get picked up. He said," Okay, good luck, your breakfast is there." Again a man of few words, but I could feel his disappointment that I was home. He had made those trips with Mom when he "was up for it" when I was at Southern, and he knew I could play, but being home now was more like he knew I was sad and disappointed and this was his way of showing or communicating that he understood, but couldn't say. What he could say, he said through his cooking, and when he cooked he cooked with love. So I dug into the plantains, cabbage, all colorful peppers, onions, sliced carrots, and mushroom-smothered liver. Yes, liver! I love liver, and he knew it. The Giants and Patriots game was about to begin, so I brought my breakfast into the living dining room area and sat at the small dining table where my brother Michael had constructed a fort again, as I sat eating and waiting for the game to begin. The meal was great as always, and after I finished, I washed it all down with purple Kool-Aid. Mom always had container of Kool-Aid of some sort in the fridge, and so my stomach was content and ready to watch the game. The game began at one o'clock and the Giants received the ball and were on offense first. When the Patriots' defense was called out in the second half, I recognized Rick was out there too. He was at left corner for the first preseason game! I was excited for him, but I was even more excited to see what he would do. I can't recall play-by-play of the game, but one play that has stayed with me all this time was the play Rick made. Rick was lined up on the left side of the field on this particular play against the Giants number one draft pick Mark Ingram Sr. Rick was lined up inside of the receiver as the receiver released outside heading up the sidelines. I don't know if the Giants coaching staff knew that there was a rookie out there by himself lined up on the number one pick and that they thought they could get away with a quick score. Maybe they did, but they didn't know what I knew about Rick and Southern football players, which was, although we played at a division two school, our skills and abilities were competitive with division one players. As Rick and Mark headed down field, side by side, Mark attempted to distance himself by accelerating and fading away from Rick on the pattern. Rick stayed right with him, keeping his eyes on him, and fading with him closer to the sideline. The ball was thrown to their side as they both reached up to catch it, and for a moment I wasn't sure who would come down with the ball. Rick was in perfect position as he reached up with his limited vertical and snatched the ball out of the air right from the grips and in front of Mark. I jumped for joy as I saw Rick come down with the ball and ran excited and jubilant to the Patriots sidelines. Making a play like that against a number one draft pick would guarantee your place on the team for at least one more week, and respite from knowing you wouldn't get that dreaded knock on the door and comfortably knowing another paycheck was coming your way. During mini camp you didn't get paid your contract money, from a few hundred thousand to the multi-millions. Every player received the same compensation during preseason, and any compensation for a rookie was good money, which was cherished as though it was a million dollars. I was happy for Rick; he was the best player on our Southern team, and he demonstrated that on that play against the best player in front of him as he had done many times before at Southern Connecticut. I don't recall anything else about that game, and I don't remember who won the game, but I do remember is Rick "California Boy" making the play.

CHAPTER SIX
TIMEOUT

My first week on waivers had passed, and there were no calls. My agent Rich called and wanted to know if I had heard anything directly from any teams that were interested in me prior to the draft like the Oakland Raiders. I told him no, and he said he would "reach out and see what's out there." He asked again if I wanted to go to Canada, and I declined again. It may have been a mistake as I look back now, but back in 1987 I was a twenty-two-year-old trying to make his way and decisions on his own and I decided to stay the course to the NFL. At this time during the broadcast there were rumors of a collective bargaining agreement conversation going on between the players union and the league. I didn't pay much attention to it; I just thought it to be another business protocol that happens in sports and business. Little did I know at that time how significant that rumor was and its effect on me that I too was going to face in weeks to come. I stayed home and trained at the high school by running the quarter mile lakes in front of the school and lifting weights at Iona College. By now all my lifting partners were back at school and/or were starting working in their fields of study. I was left alone to take this journey to the end, but I was determined to see it through. Coach Crocker was still there at Iona, and at times I would visit with him to pass the time. By now the second week had passed and I wasn't picked up. I didn't receive any calls, which I mentioned earlier was unlikely due to the roster sizes needing to be down by opening day, but I still had hoped for a call from someone who could use my skills as free safety and hitting ability. As the week passed and there was one last week left before the beginning of the 1987 season, it was announced that the NFL players were going on strike! The owners and players were at odds over medical benefits, roster sizes, and wages. As they worked out the concerns, the owners reported the season would go on. I wasn't sure what that meant initially until it was announced the teams would use *replacement players* to fill the void of the final identified roster positions for that season. What would that mean for me? Would I get a call? Well yes. At the official ending of preseason, I was called by player personnel of the Giants and asked if I wanted to come in and play while the regulars were out on strike. I contemplated at first and called Rich and asked him to explain to me what this means and if I should do it. He said, "It's a strike, and will not necessarily be looked positively on by the players," He also said, "It will give you another opportunity to show what you can do." I would be receiving my rookie contract that I signed while as a free agent that would be more than the new players coming in that were not in NFL camps prior to the strike. I called the Giants back and told them I had accepted the opportunity to come play for the Giants.

I was to report to the Giants stadium that week either Wednesday or Thursday. There was an upcoming game against the

Miami Dolphins that was questionable if it was still going to take place. Game or not, I was going to getting paid a weekly game check that most people at that time wouldn't see in an entire month. When Mom came home that night, I told her what happened and that I'd be leaving on Thursday and this would be an opportunity to make some money to get her out the apartment we were living in. She said, "Don't worry about me. I'll be fine; just feel confident and play." I called Kandice and told her too, that this would be a chance to show my skills and send her some money. The baby was still at least four months away, but I wanted to let her know that I was still trying to make it. Wednesday night, I'd called Raymond to see if he would be able to take me to the Marriot hotel in Hackensack NJ. They wanted us to report there because they anticipated protestors being out in front of the stadium. He said he would and if it would be all right to bring a lady friend along for the ride. I said, "Sure, who is it?"

"None of your business, you'll see when I pick you up," he said.

"Okay then, I'll see you in the A.M. I have to be here by noon," I said. We agreed to meet at 10:00 A.M. in front of my building, and he was there on time waiting for me with "Nay" his lady friend in the front seat. She offered up her seat to me, but Raymond in his comedic way told her not to move "for that Mfer." That was rays way of energizing the moment with an outlandish statement of an even more outlandish narrative woven into one of his comedic stories. I guess I was the joke of the day to start the day. So across the street from my building was the entrance to I-95 and so we jumped on there and headed to Hackensack, New Jersey to my new digs and the opportunity to enjoy professional football life if only for moment.

I checked into the hotel and was greeted by a familiar face, Coach Sweatman, who presided over the late-night knock on my dorm room door while in camp, along with other football staff. A brief meeting was set that evening to greet those who made it in that night, but a full meeting was scheduled for the next day Friday. The next day we met for breakfast in the hotel conference room. The wide receiver Lovelady who had NFL experience with the Redskins and was in the Giants camp with me was released after the Patriots game and he was called back too during the replacement games. There were many reasons why players played in those games. Some reasons were that they wanted to exhaust all the time they had to play the game they loved, and others, for the share amount(s) of money they were about to make, even though they knew they never had a chance to make an active roster spot in he NFL. I had all the boxes checked at this point; no money for a baby on the way, and I knew I could still play at this level of competition. I just needed another shot. Most of the players were in that night, but at the meeting the next morning there were a lot of new faces that I hadn't seen in the Giants camp, and there were those who hadn't been in any pro camp that preseason. The word out in the media was that most teams knew a strike was to happen due to the unresolved negotiations and the ongoing collective bargaining agreement discord, but some teams prepared for a strike as a safety net, while others did not. The Giants were one of those teams who didn't prepare for the 1987 NFL strike, and the outcome of their lack of preparation would be seen and unravel before all our eyes.

In the secondary we were pretty solid I thought. I was in at strong safety, out of position, but I at least knew the playbook and understood what Belichick and Parcells were looking for. JB Brown came back too. He was released in mini camp but decided to come back and give it another attempt to be recognized for his talents and catch on with a team later as well as take home an NFL paycheck. At the other corner was "Ohio State"; he too was let go but was called back to solidify the defensive backfield. Lastly there was a safety from LSU, Steve Rehage. I didn't know much about him, but he turned out to be hitter that sacrificed it all on the field. The rest of the team was small in stature and brawn. The next day some players were brought in from a semi-pro team out of New Haven, Connecticut, who were out of shape and whose skill levels were limited to that of a semi-pro team. We were looking marginal going into the first game that weekend against Miami, but fortunately the game was canceled, which granted us another week to prepare for the San Francisco 49ers on Monday night football. For as long as this opportunity would last, I was going to soak up every moment of this journey with the New York Giants. Every day we were picked up from our hotel and driven to the Meadowlands in East Rutherford, NJ, a mile or two down the road. I don't recall seeing protesting outside the stadium gates those first few days, but at some point fans protested the replacement players for coming in and filling in for the regular 49-man roster. Players had their reasons for playing during that time, and I will venture to say it was mostly financial. For me it was two-fold. The first being the new baby on the way, which was financial, and the other was to prove doubters wrong that I could play in the NFL. Now that I was here, I was official and even under these irregular conditions, at the end of the day and forever I will be in the history book as a player for the New

York Football Giants. It was good to put my helmet back on and the issued sweat pants with my number 37 on it. I felt at home. I felt that I should be here, not only now, but part of the regular 49-man roster.

Sunday we had breakfast as a group in the hotel like preseason camp and morning meetings to bring the newcomers up to speed. For me, Lovelady, Brown, and "Ohio State," it was a review and another week of reinforcement of what to do with the addition education and practice for what we had lost when we were released. We hit the field, and you could hear the same voices I had heard just a few weeks earlier in Pleasantville, New York. Parker, Leachman, with their southern drawl, and Coach Sweatman running around assisting on the field, and my favorite Romeo, always professional, supportive, and positive. I do believe they felt uncomfortable not having the regulars there and were eager to get the season going with them. I saw heads swinging from side to side, as though they were saying to themselves, "This kid can't do it." If that is what they were saying, I would tend to agree with them. The coaches played the hand they were dealt, with professionalism and respect towards us all. We would have two weeks to prepare for our first game since the schedule first game against Miami was officially suspended. The suspension set us up for our biggest moment on this journey. It not only provided us all an opportunity to put on the *big blue* uniform, but the fact that the uniform and our performance was to be showcased on primetime, on Monday Night Football on CBS. After two weeks of practice, the defense "seemed" to be prepared for the first game. Our offense with Lovelady, Crocicchia, and another good receiver, Lewis Bennett from Florida AM University, were on the outsides ready to play. Lovelady and Bennett had at least one year of NFL experience either in NFL camps or made an active roster for part of a year. As the week progressed, it appeared everyone on the defense knew their responsibilities, which is half the battle when going to war on the gridiron. The other half is execution of those responsibilities when the lights are on with forty thousand fans in the stands yelling at you and every opposing player going full speed looking to knock your head off. I wasn't sure if the Connecticut semi-pro players were up for the challenge, but that's the hand we were dealt, so that's the hand we were going to play with. As the week moved along, protesters lined the entrance gate to the stadium "welcoming" the replacement players with signs and verbal expression of the current NFL experience and the "imposter" taking the field for the football Giants. We understood the passion of the fans because not to0 long before we too were fans of the names we yearned to see running across the field. We understood that 56, 11, 58, or 89 would be out there, but at the end of the day, those that would be taking to the field on this Monday night had traveled the same mile as those that the fans wished were there. We sweat hours like the "regulars" did on the gridiron like they did. The least of the men that took the field that night are better than ninety percent than most fans that watch professional football in the comforts of their home with hot chocolate and cookies in hand. An NFL caliber player is the elitist of all athletes if you ask me. The professional football players have the traits and abilities of multiple sports like baseball, rugby, basketball, soccer, and track, compiled together to activate a cohesive and coordinated functioning machine capable of providing and an exhibition of art in motion bringing beautiful destruction on every play. The least of them that are able to put on a professional sports uniform are far above any Monday morning quarterback.

Sunday's walk through was comprehensive, but with a feeling of we're going to go out and do good with what we have." I didn't get a sense of confidence coming from the leadership and that they finally realized they left themselves (Giants) totally unprepared. The athlete's intention in spite of the administrations preparation was to give their all and to present a good quality product on the field. We were excited and confident about having the opportunity to live our dreams at the up and coming game, and we looked forward to the challenge and the Monday Night kick off.

We had our pre-game meetings Sunday night. Coach Belicheck reviewed and encouraged us to do our best, and although we were "replacing" the regulars, he expected us to give our best and reminded us we were representing the New York Football Giants organization and ourselves and should expect to be the best out there. I slept relatively well the night before, but I had some anxiety about it and I was still just twenty-two years old and inexperienced. Monday was here and we made our way over to the field by noon. It may appear to the outsider that getting to the field at noon may be too early, but actually it was perfect because you don't realize how fast time flies by, and before you know it, the whistle for kick off would be blown. The process of preparing began around two o'clock. The team would enter the stadium and walk around for a minute and taking in the atmosphere and imagining the fans screaming and yelling "Go Giants." Seeing the seats empty at two o'clock and imagining the fans cheering and booing me at seven o'clock was something I looked forward to. We had a team meeting to review responsibilities and I felt "confident" knowing what those responsibilities were. The starting defensive roster was called out. It was JB Brown, Ohio State, Steve Rehage, and Pat Morrison. I would be the starting strong safety for the Monday night football game on CBS. I wasn't shocked but realized that I would be counted on like the other ten starters to set the defensive tempo for the backups who would be getting in the game in the second half. I was trained and now was the time to lay it all on the line. The second announcement was when I was called out by team administration to do an interview with CBS in their truck parked in the tunnel. "Me!" What the heck?" Talk about pressure to perform on the field, now perform behind the mic where millions of people would be watching and listening. As a corporate communications major at Southern, I learned the business side of communications, behind the scene activities and presentations, and so I had no neither the experience nor right to get behind the microphone doing an interview. I didn't say no and went ahead and did it away. Questions started out soft, lay up questions such as, "You're from New Rochelle down the road; so how does it feel to come back home?" Easy question, and I handled with ease. But I recognized the escalation and type of questions about the game. Such as, "Who's going to win?" That's the old set up, Joe Naimeth question, and like a naïve, silly, and inexperience communicator, I fell right into to the trap. "We're going to win," I said. Predicting a win was a sin in professional sports. The only person in sports history that consistently predicted the outcome of a match was "The Greatest" Muhammad Ali, and I was no Muhammad Ali or the greatest.

My number 37 jersey sat on the hook in my locker. It was a surreal feeling that came over me at that moment. I was about to put on an official professional American football jersey, a dream I had since 1974. Did I ever really think I would be here tonight? I'm not sure if the thought was consistent throughout my life, but there were moments when others did, and saw something in me that said, "Yes, you were made for this day." Was it Principal Popolado in fourth grade? Or was it Coach Gilbride and Cavanaugh at Southern who pushed me and tested me to be better and do better because they saw more in me than I was projecting and producing myself? What or whoever got me to this point, I'm thankful for them and the opportunity to live out this dream, and this night. I recall at some point during the week, we were asked, "How do we want to get paid?" The options were weekly, which was the only way I knew people got paid, monthly, or quarterly. I asked myself, "Who gets paid quarterly, and what does that pay check look like?" I can't confirm this, but another player told me that he saw a LT's per game check that fell on the floor during camp and it was between 27-28 thousand per game! Well, my game check wasn't going to be that much, but based on my contract and my decision to get paid weekly for the sixteen-game season, I would be very content with the zeros I was about to receive. It was nearly game time, and we were dressed and ready to hit the hallway for pre-game warm up. But before we went out, Coach Belicheck came up to me and scolded me. He said my interview was inappropriate and that you should never show up the opponent. In college, athletes would talk like that, with ego, brashness, and confidence, but in the NFL, it's a no-no. The NFL is a business, and you respect the business and your colleagues even if they work on a different team (department). I got it, but his advice was futile and late. I did take that advice and used it later in life when coaching in youth football programs while coaching my son who now plays college football.

As we ran out onto the field, we could see fans in their regular seats high in the rafters away from everyone. Then there were others, hanging over the wall and railings with supporting cheers, asking for autographs and shouting "Giants, Giants, Giants!" People wanted to see football, and they wanted to see Giants football no matter who was under the helmet. It was all of our hopes that we would represent the brand with pride and distinction in spite the outcome of the night's game, and I was going to do my best to live up to the Giants brand and what it represented. After the pre-game walk through, we came back into the locker room to prepare for Monday night football to begin. We checked our uniforms, talked among ourselves a bit, while others removed themselves from the group altogether and went into seclusion preparing themselves mentally for the task at hand. As the coaches made their way around the locker room, checking and double-checking on everyone, you could feel the tension in the air as we got closer to kick off time.

CHAPTER SEVEN
GAME TIME!!!!

Up in the evening sky you could see the ball sail cross its blackness heading toward our returner signaling the opening of Monday Night Football. The kickoff returner was a little running back from Bucknell University, a small Division 1AA school located in Western, PA. After he made a successful catch of the ball, he shifted his way out to the 30-yard line where he was met with an on slot of tacklers from San Francisco. The offense started out with Croc at quarterback, Lovelady and Bennet at the wide receiver spots, with Robert Di Rico from Bucknell shuffling time with Dana More from Mississippi State and Van Williams from E. Tennessee State at the running back position. When I looked at the defensive line of the 49ers, and what our offense was about to come face to face with, there was a noticeable disadvantage. It was obvious they had more players with NFL experience, by their athletic body dimensions, which fully demonstrated that. I knew right there before the first snap that we would be in for a long battle this night. As I mentioned before, most teams prepared for the strike weeks before the first game. The Giants put together a team of the least qualified and capable football players to compete at the level of the NFL. On the first play of the game, Robert was high jacked in the backfield for a loss of three yards. As the first series progressed, the offensive line dug down and made some headway and finally moving the ball to the 49ers 45-yard line where we stalled and had to punt the ball away.

The defense was ready to go! The semi-pro defensive line was upbeat and hyped to start the game, and so was the secondary. For most the game I remember I was lined up on and towards the right side of the defense, which was equivalent to the left and strong side of the opposing offense. This meant that most running plays would be run towards the right side of the offense towards the middle with a few plays going to the left or my side of the field. That's mostly due to the fact that most people in the world are right-handed and running or throwing to their strong side is more natural to do. The first snap of the ball, the defensive line stepped up and stopped the offense for a lost. "Maybe I was wrong," I said to myself as I intensely praised my teammates for their efforts in making the play behind the line of scrimmage. After another running play, which the 49ers gained back the yards they previous lost, brought us to third down and long, which meant nine out of ten times it would be a passing play. We lined up in our based defense and cover three, zone coverage. This would be my first time playing cover three from the strong safety position where I would have to keep my head on a swivel between getting back 12-15 yards into the curl flat area and looking for a running back coming out of the back field, which is opposed to sitting nicely in the middle of the field reacting to the quarterback and breaking on the thrown ball. The third down snap went off, and I kept my head on the swivel heading to my area, 15 yards back on the field, when I noticed that it wasn't a pass at all but another running play, a draw play to be exact. The running back broke through the defensive line and scooted towards the first down, but was stopped just short by a crushing hit by Rehage up coming from his free safety position. We celebrated as we ran off the field feeling relieved and satisfied that we got out the first series of downs without any damage being done. As the game went on you could feel the intensity of the game build from a place of cautious to confidence and aggression. We all knew that our play in this game would possibly provide opportunities for some players to continue their careers for the rest of the season or even called back to the same team next season. And I was one of the players. I using this opportunity as a recruiting tool to get back on with the Giants or with another team this season or next.

The offense was back on the field and we came out throwing the ball. Lovelady and Bennett were real good receivers; unfortunately for them, their efforts to land a spot on an NFL team had fallen short up to this point. They were in NFL camps for the last two years but hadn't solidified a full roster spot, so being with the Giants this year would be their last go around before they would hit the "real" working world. Croc made great throws to Lovelady along the sidelines for first downs and the offense moved the ball past the 50-yard line into 49er territory. On the next play, we moved the ball a few more yards after a good gallop by Dana White. It was now third down and short, which commonly calls for a short running or passing play to get the first down. We all stood looking earnestly to see what the call was going to be. I looked over to Coach Parcells who was whispering something into the ear of the offensive coordinator Ron Erhardt, which could mean something unusual was about to happen. The offense broke the huddle and ran up to the ball. Croc looked over the defense as he surveyed his plans to get the first down. "Set. Hike," Croc said as he pulled away from the center to drop back to throw the ball. It was a pass, and based on his drop in he pocket, it wasn't a short one. Our excitement rose as we earnestly awaited the outcome of the whispered communications. Lovelady and Bennett streaked down the field into their patterns. As I looked up into the monitor on the south end of the field with the backdrop of the triple black sky, I could see Croc choose Bennett to receive his tightly thrown spiral down field. As Bennett and the defensive back battled for position to catch and defend, the ball came closer and closer into their vicinity, and it was time for one of them to make a play on the ball one way or another. As they sped down field and the ball drew closer to their bodies, it lost momentum, and the velocity of the ball was falling a foot short of their positions which landed on the back of the defender blocking the vision of Bennett to see the ball. But out of nowhere, you could see Bennett's hand reached around the defender's body, which was now face guarding him. Bennett tapped the ball into the air and grabbed it with his other hand as he stumbled and tip-toed his feet into the end zone for a touchdown. It was a touchdown, made by an incredible catch, which put the Giants on the board first! Obviously we felt good after the touchdown and the extra point was made, but it was still the first quarter and we still had another three and half quarters to go. I looked back at Coach Parcells and I saw a little chuckle and congratulations to the player as he looked over to Erhardt in celebration, then looking across the field to Coach Bill Walsh smiling back.

Our first score of the game left us feeling good as if we had a chance to win the game, which would be a redemption and confidence booster to the players who decided to go against the status quo and prove they belonged on the field that night. We kicked off to them again, which their receiver brought it out to the 45-yard line. That was too much return yardage after a kick off, which put us on our toes, eagerly looking to hold them form not scoring. Well, that was when the 49ers adjusted after their first series and put together a plan to run the ball down our throats. They started running the ball strategically inside of tackle holes where the semi-pro tackles were. They stood 6'3", 300 to 330 pounds, but their athletic abilities didn't match their size fro the NFL game. So San Fran ran back and forth, side to side, and at times threw the ball to the back out of the back field. I anxiously wanted to get some action, but most of the time as I got here, the running back would be heading down to the ground. I was able to make a few tackles on the opposite side of the field by anticipating that the ball would head that way, and so I did. It felt good to hit someone, another "NFL" player in a NFL game, and I can say that I came and I achieved that goal. On one tackle, my hand got caught in a player's face mask as I came high and tried to close line him, which ended up cracking a small bone in my hand. "My luck," I thought to myself as I tried to hide my pain from the trainers and my teammates.

As the game drew closer towards the end of the first quarter, the 49ers began throwing the ball down field. On a second down play, the quarterback dropped back to throw. As I headed back into my zone in cover three, I saw him looking towards my side of the field. He took a deep drop back, which meant he was going deep with his throw. As I put my head on a swivel heading towards my zone and saw that no running back was heading into the flat side lines, I broke off my responsibility and trailed JB, the cornerback from Miami who had the receiver covered like a blanket. As a rookie you can appreciate those players who have had experience in the NFL; it was a moment to watch and learn. JB was calm and running stride for stride with the replacement receiver along the sideline. The ball drew closer to them, and as the receiver looked up for the ball so did JB, leaning against him with his back, while raising his right arm and hand and punching the ball away. I witnessed perfect execution on how to cover a receiver down field. I trailed the play with hope to get a deflection and interception if the ball would deflect my way, but it didn't. JB punched the ball way out of bounce into the 49ers sidelines. Although that was a great play, the 49ers over the next couple of plays slowly moved the ball down the field and scored on an off tackle run to tie the score. The score was tied up after the extra point going halfway through the second quarter. After the kickoff, the offense moved the ball with passes and runs but turned the ball over on downs, which meant the 49ers would have a chance to score again before the end of the quarter heading into halftime. The second play of the quarter, the quarterback dropped back looking in my direction to throw the ball. As I dropped back into my curl to flat drop, I noticed the big full back Verajon slide out to the wing awaiting the swing pass to him. I recognized it early and made my way towards him ready to make the tackle, which would cost them to lose yardage. The ball was thrown to Verajon and as I came up to make the tackle, when the wide receiver to my side of the field made a "cracked back" block and hit me in my back causing me to be out of position to make a good tackle and forcing me to reach out with my injured hand in an attempt to tackle him. I was able to get my arm to hit his leg as he galloped towards the line of scrimmage, but that wasn't enough as he stumbled forward for five yards before falling and being covered up by JB. I was pissed because that was an opportunity to make a solid solo play and add a tackle to my portfolio for the coach to comment on positively. That didn't happen, but I was saved because the "crack block" was seen by the referees and a penalty flag was thrown. As I made my way back to the huddle, I heard the referees say, "Illegal block to the back, clipping." I thought I was saved because the 49ers didn't make any yards and they would actually lose yards. Not the case because I was substituted with my back-up. When I ran and returned to the sidelines, Coach Parcells called me over with a scowl on his face, and he said, "What you doing? Stop being scared and make the tackle!"

"Scared!" I said out loud. At that moment I forgot about any protocol as a player to keep my mouth shut and be quiet and the old "Pat Morrison/Hollywood" came out. "The crazy Bunch" Pat Morrison. And in an attempt to explain that I was clipped by the wide receiver, I was pulled away by Lovelady and told to "relax and take a seat." Belichick came over and said, "Pat, you have to make that play." I told him what happened, but he knew by now because the play was called back. The quarter was coming to an end, but the 49ers began moving the ball down the field and came within field goal range, which they took advantage of and kicked a field goal with two minutes left in the half, and the score now being 10-7. With two minutes left in the half, all we had to do was to hold onto the ball and go into the half, down three points.

We received the kickoff and went out to keep the ball on the game to run the ball out for the half. What happened next took the wind out of our sail. On a handoff to DiRico up the middle, he made it through the front line but fumbled into the secondary and recovered by the 49ers. There was enough time remaining on the clock for them to score, but it would be encouraging if the defense could hold them and keep that three-point difference. The 49ers used the clock wisely and recognized that our big boys up front were tired. Their conditioning was poor and hadn't had enough time with the Giants program to get in NFL shape. They got into the red zone and they came out late out of the huddle, and I had to scamper to find their strong side to line up. I lined up on the strong side, but after one cadence they moved the tight end from one side to the other which caused me to move with him as simultaneously the ball was snapped going the other way. A mixed direction play was called which led to a touchdown over the right side away from me. After the extra point cleared the up-rights, we were now down 17-7 at the half and an entire half yet to go, bad hand and all.

We got into the locker room, and angry voices filled the air. We all knew we were playing relatively well but let up and allowed the 49ers to get back into the game and build confidence at the end. Lovelady was upset and boisterous in his attempt to encourage everyone to keep their heads up and stop making silly mistakes on the offense so they can take advantage of match ups. The defense was doing relative okay, but our play towards the end of the quarter was due to conditioning. Playing in an NFL is more than physical. The energy of the stadium, the fans, and the intensity is at another level that cannot be practiced unless you come form a power 5 school who plays in front of 80-100 thousands fans every week. Coming from Southern Connecticut, a small division two school, I could feel the difference of energy and intensity that I felt fully. Belichick pulled the defensive over and called out the defensive front line for not doing a better job of shutting down the running lanes and not creating a new line of scrimmage in the backfield. However, it didn't appear that he was fully disappointed because I believe his expectations were not that high for the team he was handed. After a couple of minutes with the defense, we were separated into our position coaches. Coach Fontes provided limited feedback about our play, but he did say I should recognize the play sooner in the flats and beat the crack-back block. I'm thinking to myself, "Damn, I went through my reads, broke on the ball, and nearly made the play before I got hit in the back." Oh well, I didn't let it bother me and listened to the rest of the instructions before we were dismissed. I went over and picked up two Gatorades. I knocked those down, and I went over to my locker and sat there quietly as I listened to the rumblings amongst the other players in the locker room. Croc was a motivator. He went around trying to encourage everyone to keep their heads up and "come out in the second half and win this game." I was with him all the way, as well as having that burning desire to be "good enough" and to see it through to the end, and allow the coaches to see and know that I should be here. The trainer, Ronnie Barnes, came over to check out my hand and asked if I was okay. "Let me take a look at it," he said, and I replied, "I'm okay; it hurts a bit, but I'll be fine."

After pressing and some slight manipulating, he said, "You have a small fracture above your thumb."

"Okay, tape it up, and I'll be fine," I said. I went over to the training area, got taped up, and was ready to go back out. Before we headed back out unto the field, the trainers provided report to the coaches that listed the "injured and hurt." Unfortunately I was one that injured. That was the last thing I wanted the coach to hear. Although I played decent in the first half, I really didn't do anything to impress the coaches, and the block in back eclipsed the one solo opportunity I had, which Coach Parcells thought I just clearly missed. A few minutes before we went out for the second half, Coach Belichick came to me and told me that he was replacing me at strong safety in the second half. I was devastated because I believed that it was something I did or something I didn't do. I realized there were other players brought in whom they wanted to give an opportunity to play in the game. I was placed on special teams, running down on kickoffs.

Second half was about to start, and we got together as a unit for a moment of "ra-ra" moment and encouragement. As we walked through the hallway towards the tunnel to run out onto the field, I didn't have the same feeling of excitement as I did at the beginning of the game. I felt that anger from years past come over me, and I wanted to let it out on someone immediately. We ran out onto the field and ran out full steam ahead. As I ran out, I could hear the twenty or so thousand fans cheering us on, which was encouraging knowing that real fans don't cheer on players per se, but rather they cheer and root for the colors and their home team, and tonight we; the replacement players were their home team. As I sat on the sidelines, stretching and loosening up, Coach Belicheck came over and said, "You'll play the first couple of series before I put the next guy in." I was like "cool" in my head. I never showed outward emotions in front of the coaches, but inside I was like "bet." We kicked off to the 49ers in the second half where I was placed on kickoff, which allowed me more game time and time on the field. The ball was kicked off, and the returner returned the ball out to the thirty-five yard line and that was much too much yardage on a kickoff, which always puts a defense on its heals. As I lined up again in our cover three, I recognized the change in quarterbacks by the 49ers. At present the quarterback was Stevens, who was a Canadian experienced pro football player originally from Passaic, New Jersey. The first play Stevens ran was a quarterback off tackle keeper out of the wishbone offensive setting. The wishbone is an offense scheme only seen in college football. Coach Walsh implemented this scheme I guess to add a little excitement and experimentation. After the play you could see Parcells and Walsh acknowledge the scenario as they chucked at each other across the field again. The 49ers were playing to win. Like I said before, most teams prepared better than the Giants for the strike, and it showed as Stevens played the rest of the game, rushing for thirty-six yards and a touchdown run, threw two passes, one for thirty-nine yards and a touchdown and all out of the wishbone formation. We continued to struggle throughout the game offensively and defensively, and by the second series of the second half I was no longer playing on defense and awaiting opportunities to go down on kickoff. The Giants ended up losing the game to the 49ers, forty-one to twenty-one, 41-21. We entered the locker room disappointed and discouraged. I don't believe because we lost the game but it was more to do with how we loss the game. Our linemen were caught on big screen gasping for air on the sidelines and another looked like he was taking a nap. It was also embarrassing. As we listened to Coach Parcells's final words for the evening, it appeared as though he wasn't really pressed by the loss. The Giants were behind the players and the players union on the strike, so it's understandable to some extent about the lack of anger outward expressed by him and others. It also reinforces the Giants' administration's lack of effort to go out and field a competitive team. After the game, after showers and putting on our dress to go out for the night, I received my "brown envelope." As a player you have an option to receive your game compensation in different ways. A player can receive his paycheck after the game, bi-weekly, monthly, or in some cases quarterly. Well, me being in this peculiar situation with the strike, as well as only knowing one way to be compensated for a week's work, was to ask for my pay directly after the game. I knew what my contract was, but I never calculated what it would be like after taxes and the nine dependents I put down on my W-2 form. Most players put down multiple dependents to retain most of their money, with no fair of the IRS. As I walked out into the hallway heading towards the charter buses and opened my brown envelope, I had never seen that many zeros for a week's worth of work! Growing up in New Rochelle, many of us had summer jobs working at various sites throughout the city, sponsored by the government that taught us skills in construction, life guard skills, etc. and work ethic, which I really appreciated, and at the end of the two-week period you received couple hundred dollars that made you think you hit the lottery or something. But looking at this check that I received just after one-week employment was foreign and downright criminal in itself for a twenty-one-year-old to receive. I took my check, folded it in half, and placed it in my front pocket for safekeeping. When we got back to the hotel, we all went to our rooms and called it a night.

The next morning we got up bright and early to start our day. Breakfast was held in the hotel, and afterwards we made or way over to the stadium, where we once again we were greeted by protesters with signs with the words "scab" written on them. Just seeing the word "scab" brought about an array of feelings that stemmed from shame to anger. The protocol in the NFL is that the day directly after the game you play, which is Monday, you practice. In college you play on a Saturday, rest on Sunday for film review in evening, and it's back on the field on Monday. In the NFL you do all of the above on the day after the game; we watch film, where you get chewed out for an hour about your play. Then we hit the field for a mild walk through and review. It's not meant to be a brutal full practice, but a relaxed practice to get the blood flowing again and to follow up with the trainers to address injuries. My hand overnight had swollen up above the thumb area, and I was having a hard time gripping the ball. The medical staff took a look at it and said it may be broken, but they wouldn't know without an x-ray was taken. We practiced for the rest of the week with no day off because it was a short week with the Washington Redskins coming in to town for a Thursday night game. I was looking forward to competing in this game for two reasons: one being that I now had one game under my belt and having the NFL experience, even though modified, would help me going into game two. I did get an education of what is expected of me from the coaches, the speed of the game, and the overall aura of the stadium experience. Two being that being on the field with one of my college teammates, Mark Carlson, who too was a free agent before the season and crossed the line to play in the replacement games. Mark played offensive tackle at six foot six and three hundred and thirty pounds. When he first came to Southern, Mark came in as a transfer tight end from Boston University. Getting to line up opposite him again would be good, exciting, and interesting as I gave him a couple of licks back at Southern that would jolt his memory when he'd see me coming off the edge. I don't recall too much about that week of practice that led up to the game, but by Wednesday I felt something was wrong. I was officially put on special teams and replaced as strong safety. It wasn't made clear why I was not starting, but I figured the coaches wanted to give other players the opportunity to play and have their moment to shine. It didn't bother to me as much as I thought it would because as long as I was on the field, I would be satisfied to be in the game.

As game time rolled around on Thursday, I was ready to play and do my part as the team tried to bounce back from the dismal Monday night loss against the 49ers. The usual protocol was in place: eat early dinner at the hotel and make our way over to the stadium by four o'clock. After we came in and put our belongings down in our lockers, we journeyed out as usual to walk the field and take in the solemn moment and await the cheers and tears of fans sitting in the scarcely populated stadium seats. After an half-hour of absorbing the atmosphere and imagining the sounds of the upcoming night and picturing myself in my coverages and making plays, I turned and made my way back towards the tunnel heading towards the locker room, when I was stopped by one of the assistant coaches/equipment managers who informed me I was *inactive* for the game. My stomach fell to the ground, and it felt like I was stabbed in the heart at the same time. " Like why?" I said to myself. I know my assignments, I hustled to the ball, I try to get in on all the plays, and I only had one ball caught on me that was called back for clipping. "So why?" My chances to prove to myself and the Giants grew slim as my anxiety and rage grew inside. I made my way into the locker room and saw that my jersey and equipment weren't there, which could mean it was a last minute decision and why my equipment was removed at the last minute. Either way it didn't sit well with me, one because I wanted to play, and two, my friends in New Ro, like Icky, Angelo, and Coach Crocker were expecting to see me play. I felt like I let them down and my city. Lovelady came over to me and asked me, "Why aren't you getting dressed, dude?" I told him I was inactive for the game, which threw him for a loop, which left an expression of frustration on his face. Even Lovelady felt some sort of way about me not playing in the nights game, and because he knew me from mini camp and he knew what I was capable of doing if only given the opportunity to show. Although my hand was in pain still, I believe it may have been an excuse to keep me out of the game and have other players play. An hour before the game, we had our team and position meetings where Coach Belicheck doubled down on the decision that I would be inactive for the night's game. A few of us were inactivated for the game, as we stood on the sidelines watching the football sail through the triple black night sky again at kickoff. I don't remember the particulars of the game, maybe because I subconsciously blocked out the night because of my disappointment and the decision to sit me down. All I remember is that we lost that game too. The

"Skins" was another team that prepared well for that moment in NFL history. There were many players with multiple years of NFL experience behind them, and it showed by their mere presence on the field that night and for the rest of the season. My college teammate Mark was on the offensive line looking massive, but what I saw his time out there wasn't limited to size alone but also the depth of Washington's roster they had in place. Washington went on to win the Super Bowl that year behind the first African American in a Super Bowl, Doug Williams from Grambling University, an HBCU (Historical Black College) located in Grambling, Louisiana. Mark and I had a brief encounter as we met in the middle of the field, passing along pleasantries and congratulations on Washington's win. He asked me about my hand, which he saw was wrapped from the white medical tape around my thumb and hand. I told him what happened, and he wished much luck and get better soon as we walked away and left each others space as we shook hands with other players as a show of sportsmanship.

After the game, we came in for the short after the game speech from Belichick and Parcells that I felt was half-heartfelt. I could be wrong, but once again, their positions were not ones of urgency and immediacy and those who needed to improve, be better, and do better. I felt it was more of that they knew who they had (which was less than top tier athletes across the board) and were being indifferent to that fact. The 38-12 loss was embarrassing to accept as a fan and as a player as I looked up into the stands and saw the brown paper bags lay in the aisles of the stadium with the word SCAB written on them. It was a painful moment in my career because although I looked at the opportunity to play during this unsettling time, it was a period to show my worth. A feeling of delusion came across my senses as to why would I place myself in such a circumstance that I cared so much for, but the leadership that asked me to give all of what I had to give, didn't. Even the contents of the brown envelope had less value knowing that the "job" wasn't getting done and I wasn't part of the work force to make a difference in the outcome. I took my check, folded it up, and placed it in my front pocket for safekeeping, then sat in my locker and waited for the call to get on the bus. The football Giants to his point was 0-4. The first two games of the season were played by the regulars, who lost to Chicago and Dallas respectfully. Going into week six (because of the cancelation of the Miami game) the organization didn't want to go to far down in the rankings, and any potentially any playoff opportunity that might present itself once the strike was over would be lost. The lost to the Skins was a call to the regulars to reevaluate their stance on the ongoing negotiations with the NFL, which launched conversations throughout the league that some players were considering crossing the line. Dallas had already had players cross the line, such as Tony Dorsett, Randy White, and rumors of Ed "Too Tall" Jones coming back too. Going into the next week, we had Buffalo coming up, and after the protocol day of practice after a game and day off, Sunday was here and four additions to the team was at practice: LT, Jeff Hostetler, Jeff Rutledge, and Adrian White. They all had different reasons for coming back, some financial, and some couldn't see their championship team go 0-4 after such and incredible 1986 season the year before.

I knew Adrian was back, and I thought for sure I would be sent home, because we had enough safeties in both positions now.

I wasn't sent home, and that was a relief, which also meant another paycheck was coming my way after the next game. Steve Ruhage stayed at free safety, JB and Ohio State were at the corner positions, and Adrian would be at his regular position, strong safety. I would be Adrian's back-up along with the other safety. It felt good for all of the camp guys to get back together. It was strange sitting there and wondering what it would have been like as rookies coming in, coming up, playing, and hanging out with each other all the time. Adrian, Lovelady, Bennett, and I got along well and we fed off each other every day for the next week to better each other during practice for the upcoming game against buffalo.

My hand was healing nicely with limited pain. The week of practice went well with Adrian leading the way in drills and reps. In the locker room, LT was the center of attention. He was engaging and embracing of the replacement players. I don't particularly know why he was so accommodating, but possibly because he was there like most of us there, crossing the Labor Union line solely for economic reasons. On the outside f the stadium, the protesters were not as brass as they were when the strike had first started, and possibly due to the fact, reports were coning out stating "movement" was being made in the negotiations between owners and players. When we heard that, we knew that our time was going to up sooner than later; we felt we just needed to hang on as long as we could to get these last checks and leave the regulars in a position to save the season and have a run at a playoff spot. As we prepared for the game in Buffalo, I was informed on a Friday that I would not be traveling to Buffalo on Saturday. Disappointed again, but I understood exactly why I wasn't traveling, and basically the travel team can only consist of a limited amount of players, so with the two quarterbacks, LT and Adrian, coming back, certain decisions had to be made for who would go and who would remain behind. The decision also spoke volumes of what Coach Parcells and Belichick thought of me as a player, I thought. Maybe I wasn't good enough to land a spot in the NFL permanently? Maybe I needed more practice and refinement. None of this was told to me by them, but by now your mind starts wondering and thinking for itself and why am I not traveling, and at least as a back up. My ranking coming out of college was the twentieth best safety in college in all divisions, with the number one safety being Charles Woodson the future Hall of Famer. It didn't sit well with me and I found myself questioning and asking myself that question my mother would always ask: "Are you confident enough?" At this time, I wasn't feeling too confident or competent and I just wanted to go home after my next check. I remember watching the game in my hotel room that weekend since I wasn't traveling. Both teams looked bad, even with the returning starters on offense and the premier linebacker of all time, the team still couldn't do much. There was no continuity, coordination, and sense of urgency. Out on the field there was one New York Giants that I knew growing up in New Rochelle; it was an illusion, a figment, and imitation of the Giants, and a poor one at that. And yes, I blame the Giants leadership for not taking the situation more seriously by *not* keeping the fans in mind when putting the team together. The true home team fan route for their home team in spite of who's under the helmet. Giants' fans route the New York Football Giants, Big Blue, who are expected to win, but we lost again to the Buffalo Bills that sunny Sunday afternoon by the score of 3-6. It was decided over the weekend during that game that the strike would be over and the regulars would be returning the following week.

CHAPTER EIGHT
Kirby

The term "scab(s)" was first used in the labor force context during the 1770(s) towards workers who crossed picket lines to the take the place of striking "bootmakers" in Philadelphia. The word's origins go as far back to 1250, in which it was used to describe a disease of the skin, which in return infers the word "scab" as an insult of ugliness. There is much more to the word "scab(s)" when put into context and where it is used. The Chinese who built the great railroads connecting the east and west were called "scabs" too. Today we benefit from their labor that consequently allows Americans to travel from New York to the shores of California. We get amnesia about this time in history either purposefully or unconsciously by those who write history to purposefully leave out of the curriculum actual facts to keep the "common folks" at odds, while demeaning and defacing each others humanity. The Chinese were brought in to complete the job that "Americans" didn't want to do. The capitalists at the time were keeping the nation a float with industry and providing jobs and opportunity during the Depression Era. America was in a depression and to complete the railroad construction would not only, yes fill the pockets of the industrialist, but also open additional access for trading opportunities along the train path through states throughout the Midwest. So the term "scabs" in context and at a specific time has it place. In this context, the "scab" kept the " train" rolling during a time of homelessness, helplessness, and hopelessness, and in conjunction with the conflict, disagreement and ugliness of labor strike at the time. The strikes, if we like them or not, provided the "replacement" Chinese worker an opportunity to work when there was none, and to fill a void that was left open by others who wanted more for their efforts during the nations crisis. The Chinese "scabs" worked and crossed the picket lines to make a better life for him/herself for the total benefit of us all then and in the future.

We were asked to return to the stadium Monday for our last meeting and to collect anything we may have left in our lockers that we wanted to take with us. I didn't have much left in my locker but some turf shoes, socks, gloves, and wristbands. We headed over to the stadium as usual for our last goodbye, and surprisingly there were no fans outside waiting with scab signs or yelling. It felt weird; reality had set in for many who participated in these games because it would be the last time they would ever experience the life of an professional athlete, and be compensated as well as we were. We all gathered in the meeting room, as we all, coaches and players, passed around salutations and best wishes. In the short five weeks' time, we all met and engaged with someone different that we probably would not have encountered any other time and possibly learned a few things from. That's one thing I'm grateful about sports; it brings people from all walks of life together, cultures and race with one common goal, to compete in athletic battle and win. We understand we can't achieve our goals unless we all work together in cooperation, unison, and continuity to achieve a common goal. We didn't win, but the memories of the journey will last a lifetime. Coach Parcells informed us what to expect for the remainder of the season which included the replacement players left on the roster for he remainder of the season, and to update us on any awards and compensation to be given to the regular players, including any playoff game compensations won, along with division championship compensation and Super Bowl appearance compensation. We were entitled to all moneys for the rest of the season. So although our time had come to an end after four weeks, we had hoped that the regulars would come in and perform like the Super Bowl Champions of 1986. Unfortunately that was not the case. The 1986 football Giants were just that, a team of the past, and the 1987 Giants was a different team, under different circumstances with different outcomes. The team ended with a 6-9 record and missed post-season opportunities to play further and pick up any extra compensation.

I was home for about a week when I received calls from some of the guys I was in camp with. Adrian and Odessa checked in with me, and we talked about coming back and how the season looked going forward. No one really knew what to expect or how eventually the team would do, but in the meantime we were planning on riding it out together, whether I was in East Rutherford/Hackensack, New Jersey or New Rochelle, NY.

Odessa invited me to a birthday party of one of the running back's on the team. I was to pick him up at his hotel where he was staying. Most of the rookies hadn't brought a home or moved

PATRICK A. MORRISON, MSW

into apartments yet because of the strike interfering with their personal schedules, but when I got there he was ready to go as we headed into the city to a nightclub where the birthday party was being held. When we entered the club, we were ushered to seats in the middle left of the lounge area with a clear view of the performing stage. It was live entertainment for the evening and the first of my adult life outside of church to witness. Performing that night was homegrown New Jersey talent that really set the house on fire. We got to the party a little after the opening so we missed the introductions and missed the names. But by the end of the night while during the last call for drinks they mentioned the names of "Ann-Marie and CC." I said, "Ann-Marie, where have I heard that name before?" Just about a week earlier I met a girl from Co-Op City in the Bronx who attended college in North Carolina and asked if I knew "Ann-Marie." I told her no, and I asked her "why?" She knew I was playing for the Giants and she knew the local towns and cities where many of the players stayed in the area of the stadium like Secaucus, Hackensack, and Paterson, New Jersey, and she wanted to know if I met her and told me she was a singer that went to school with her and that they were friends. So when I heard the name, I couldn't believe it was the same person, a coincidence to say the least. As I sat there and watched Ann-Marie finish her set, she took a seat at the table right in front of me. I was nervous because she was a big star in the 80s (I didn't know) and I wasn't sure how she would react towards someone she didn't know. I leaned over and said, "Hello, I'm a friend of Debbie." Ann-Marie immediately turned around and with a bright smile said, "That's my friend. How is she?" I said good, but we couldn't continue talking at the moment

116

because fans and colleagues were hounding her. As I sat there and listened to the other acts, the MC for the night recognized the evening as "The running back's birthday party" and wanted "any other Giants in the building to stand and be recognized."

"Does that include me?" I thought to myself. I was officially still on the team, so I just went with it and stood up. It felt good to be recognized as a NY Giant football player even if it was only on paper. After a round of applause from the crowd, the party resumed, and the conversations and mingling amongst the crowd continued. Ann-Marie turned around and officially introduced herself to me as we talked about our mutual friend. After a half hour or so and the night winding down, she offered her number to follow up with her if I needed anything down the road. It was a good night hanging out with the guys, singing, dancing, and I met a "star" who gave me her number to "follow up with her." After the party, I got ready to drive Odessa and Stephen back to the hotel. We laughed all the way back to the hotel as I talked about the evening, catching up on the season, and learned different foods from Louisiana, like Boudin. Boudin is a Cajun sausage from Louisiana that resembles a small hot dog. Stephen and I cracked jokes on Odessa's Louisiana slang accent and food choices all the way back to Hackensack.

After I dropped them off, I had a feeling of loneliness knowing how much I was missing the camaraderie of my teammates and missing out on the late night conversations in our rooms about the day's events. Teammates, may it be on the sports fields, basketball courts, or battleground, teamwork, and concept of teammates and the created friendships should not be underestimated. I drove my Toyota Supra, which I leased back home to New Ro, and made my way up to the same apartment on the 5th, number 12. I felt a little depressed about my situation, but I didn't start looking for employment yet because I had money in my account and had plans to move my mother out of the apartment into a house soon as I could. In the meantime I sat home and hung out with Icky, Matt, and Angelo, who was now coaching football at Iona College with Coach Crocker. For the next couple of months, I stayed in shape by working out at Iona and at the high school running and lifting weights. At this time I was maintaining one hundred and ninety pounds and relatively the best all around shape in my life. Kandice and I were still talking, off and on, but we maintained a good relationship and communication as she grew closer to her due date in January. It was December now, and I was running the streets, spending money and living free, without an income. I was hoping the team would at least make the playoffs, but the regulars didn't perform much better than we did losing nine games. Christmas season was upon us, and I split my time between Connecticut, New York, and New Jersey. I even attended some performances Ann-Marie invited me to and watch her perform in places like the Underground, Club 88, and Bentley's. She even gave me a few working gigs as her security at some of her performances. It was appreciated for the time I was away from football, maybe short, but it was a good time as I waited to figure out what my next move would be.

I may not be sure the next events outlined in this paragraph are in sequential order, but I would say during this time while waiting to make the right move, one of two accurate and significant events happened. One was the birth of my daughter London, and the other was obtaining employment at Macy's flagship store in New York City.

I was called early in the morning on January 13th, 1988 by Kandice letting me know she was heading to the St. Raphael's hospital soon and that she wanted me to be there. I wanted to be there too! But I was scared and didn't know what to expect or what to do when I got there. So I got up, took a shower, grabbed a banana, and went into Mom's room in the back of the apartment and let her know "the baby is coming and I'm heading to Connecticut." She was happy and told me to stay by Kandice's side for support. The ride up the Merritt felt longer than usual. Thoughts were going through my mind as to what say to her, her mother, and other family members who might be there, and who the baby would look like. Kandice and I were on shaky grounds to a point, and I'm wasn't sure either one of us knew where our relationship was going and what the future held for us now with a new life in our care to take care of and nurture. I arrived to the hospital by seven-thirty in the morning, and I was directed to the room where Kandice and her mother were. The first thing that came out of her mother was, "You're a father." I said, "Really?" I didn't think the baby would be here that quick because I was told she was heading to the hospital to have the baby at 2:34 in the morning, which means when I received the call by Kandice, she was actually ready to give birth. When I walked over to the bed where Kandice was holding the baby, and I looked down into her beautiful brown face, I melted at her beauty and her peace being in her mother's arms. She looked just like me, just a couple shades lighter than mine, which represented her mother's African American and Irish DNA. So I asked Kandice, "Did you pick a name?"

And she said, "Yes, London."

I said "As in London, England where I was born?"

"Yes," she said, which at that moment and time a brighter smile came across my face. I said thank you as my visit continued into the afternoon. I drove back home, the fifty-nine minutes it takes to get from New Haven to New Rochelle thinking about this responsibility I now had on my hands. I found myself in a life abyss not knowing what to do or where to go next. I was only twenty-two years old, and my football career wasn't over yet, and New Haven wasn't my home; New Ro was. I was a father now, but I hadn't yet fully embraced the title at the same time because I believed I had too much yet to do or at least try to do. I wanted to exhaust every opportunity I had or would have before I entered the reality of real world issues of work and family. I took the part-time job at Macy's where I worked in the stock room. It was decent working there, and I had the opportunity to meet a lot of people of influence, as I would walk the floors, delivering and packing shelves with clothes and accessories.

During the next couple of months, I started looking with my mother for a home in New Rochelle. I had ideas outside of New Rochelle like Harlem, where the square footages were low and real estate prices were outrageously low. I recognized this would be a prime time to get into the market and purchase something that would grow in value and be amongst the "people" of history and heritage. Mom had brought years earlier a real estate audio package from Carlton Sheets. She always had a home and property appreciation that she learned from her mother and kin, living in Jamaica. They understood that land ownership was the way out of dependence on others and that she should build or own her own. She had already purchased land in a place called Sleepy Hollow Lake in the Catskills of New York within two years of her coming to America, but she really had no way of maintaining the property due to her minimal financial gains in employment over the years and was not yet savvy to look at it as a viable venture to be in with now my limited funds. I looked to purchase a brownstone town house in Harlem, which in a few years would gain solid appreciation and would still be near by new Rochelle to maintain her church family, but Mom wanted to stay in New Ro, close to her friends and church family without interruption. My brother was still young and so she didn't want to uproot him to find new friends in a new area and a new school, which I understood completely. New Rochelle was a special place, as I have mentioned before. A city diverse in communities of race, culture, nationality, religions, and we all played and learned at one of the highly decorated school systems not only in the State of New York, but in the entire country. After conversations and thoughts, we believed to leave New Ro wouldn't necessarily be an advantage but possibly a disadvantage, especially for my brother Michael. I decided to look for a job to keep me busy while I figured out my next move. I looked through the daily newspapers, the local standard Star newspaper but didn't find much. The economy wasn't doing that well, and crack and crime were on the rise. I went back and forth between New Haven and New York, spending time with London and providing time for Mom to spend time with her too. Eventually, in one week I received couple of calls from prospects, and one of the prospects being *Essence Magazine*, the African American woman-issued publication. Getting a call back from them was exciting and welcoming. The other prospect was with a "product marketing company." I was interested and excited about the upcoming Essence interview because it all came about by a co-worker at Macy's that was from Mt. Vernon (sister city of New Ro) who referred me to her sister, who was Terri Williams, the Director of Communications at the time. The meeting and interview were set up at the main NYC office. I wasn't sure what to wear, but I found one of my old reliable church suits to wear and to present my best foot forward.

Metro North was across from our apartment so I took the train to Grand Central Station and jumped into a cab heading up town to Broadway. I got to the NYC and the interview, fifteen minutes early, on time and I was ready to go. I believe I had an "air" of confidence about me that made me feel I was capable of doing whatever job was offered to me in the communication space, but what that would look like and how much I would get paid, I had no clue. I waited ten minutes in the beautiful aesthetics of the hallway as I watched the black faces walk in and out of offices while conducting their business before I was called into Ms. Williams's office. "Mr. Morrison? Follow me please. Ms. Williams will see you now." I was greeted with a warm smile and firm handshake as Ms. Williams sat down to review my potential employment with *Essence Magazine*. We briefly talked about my relationship with her sister at Macy's and what I had done and what I was doing now. The meeting lasted about forty-five minutes or so, and by the end, Ms. Williams offered me a position in her department, the communications department. A smile skirted across my face as the news sunk in my head and I was thrilled to have secured my first "professional worldly job" on my first interview. She said someone would call me this week to go over salary and start date. I thanked her for her time and was on my way back to New Ro on Metro North. When I returned home, I ran upstairs to tell Mom, but when I walked to her room, she was already in bed sleeping and getting ready for her overnight job at the nursing home. Dad wasn't home either, so I just go undressed and settled in to watch television and eat my dinner. Mom like usual left my dinner dished out on top of the stove, on top of a pot of water to warm up. The night's dinner was rice and peas, baked chicken, and cabbage, topped off with good old Heinz ketchup made the night complete.

The next couple of days were slow and uneventful as I waited to hear back from *Essence Magazine*. Until I got that call I still had another call to make, as a back up. I received the call back from Essence by the end of the week and an offer was made with and immediate start date. "Seventeen thousand dollars, per year!" I said to myself as I listened closely to the woman on the other end of the line. I made that much in one month playing football, and my ego at the time said to me, "I deserve more than that." It's really interesting how immaturity, ego, and outright stupidity can cloud a person's cognitive process. I wasn't thinking long-term; I was thinking short-term, today and not my future. I wasn't thinking I could work my way up through and up in the company, and I didn't have the full comprehension of having the door opened to me to one of the most popular Black publications on the market where I could hone my professional "real world" skills that would serve me well in the future well after football. I believed at the time that I still had a great opportunity waiting for me with the marketing company, which after the first call said I'd have the opportunity to make as much money as I can based on how much I put in. Little did I know what that was going to be and what would turn out to be. So I turned down the job at Essence, which triggered a call from Terri Williams trying to convince me to take the position and that it would be good thing for me. She wasn't pushy, and she admitted the salary was pretty low, but indirectly she was telling me to get in, do good work, and other positions will open up later. "Hard head makes for a soft behind." I was hard-headed, and my a** was later kicked after calling the marketing company.

I was also anxious about being able to support Kandice and London. I knew that my football career, although not over, would be for a limited time, and already one year was down with one or two years left to catch on with a team. I really wasn't sure what to do. Mom didn't understand the dynamics of professional sports. She only knew hard labor work with what God has given you "two hands and two feet and a brain." My stepdad wasn't around for guidance or suggestions during my decision making process, so I made the decision(s) based on my own understanding. I had to make something happen as I thought to myself, and I had to make something happen fast! I was spending and wasting money that I made playing football, now going out to clubs, buying clothes, and running back and forth to New Jersey and hanging out with "new friends" I made.

I called the marketing company and set up an appointment for the following week in he Bronx. The meeting was set for the late afternoon to come into the Bronx office. The Bronx in the eighties wasn't really a welcoming place to be during the crack epidemic and violence. 241st Street and White Plains Road in the evening dressed in my Sunday suit was definitely a standout in the area. I parked my new Supra down the street because I couldn't find a spot near the entrance to the building I was to enter. When I got there I knew something was up because there was no sign "real sign" on the door, no "So-and-So Marketing Company." I made my way in into the space and entered through a door with no sign on it where I saw others sitting in a sparsely decorated room with no windows. There was a reception desk with a pleasant Hispanic female receptionist siting behind a glass window directing me to fill out an employment application. As I sat in the far corner of the room, I looked around and scoped out my surroundings and evaluated the other potential employees for the job I was there to apply for. I sat there for a half-hour when a sharply dressed Hispanic male walked out and introduced himself as the local director of the company. At the time I couldn't recall the name of the company, but when he started talking he sounded like a used car salesman I remembered back in New Haven, Connecticut at the Toyota dealership. He spoke about all the money we could make and the endless opportunity to move around and up in the company to a manager, regional manager and even regional director. All these titles sounded great and the potential money opportunities were enticing and sounded great, but I still didn't know what the job was. After his fifteen-minute spiel, out came a Caucasian man with a crisp white starched shirt, tan skin, and white teeth you could see from across the street. After his welcoming pleasantries and salutations, he introduced himself to the eager members of the room to the job and the marketing product.

Kirby vacuum cleaner! I'm thinking to myself that a week before I left a beautiful office building downtown Manhattan with beautiful women walking around at an international company for this, as I sat there and listened to "shiny tooth." I thought I didn't have any other options at the moment, so I sat there listened and decided to stick it out.

I trained on the Kirby vacuum cleaner for a week. In actuality, it was three days in the office. After my three days with this heavy monstrosity, we hit the hardcore streets of the Bronx, New York on a selling spree. Before the regional manager and I went out, he showed me how to "cold call," how to generate referrals and opportunities to present the machine. I scheduled two appointments that week, and by Friday we went out to demonstrate the great wonders of the Kirby vacuum cleaner. I remember one presentation scheduled that when I arrived, it was in a high-rise tenement building. I had to carry the machine up three flights of stairs to the apartment, and by the time we got there my shirt was out of my pants and my church suit was wrinkled trying to hold everything together. The manager wasn't helping out me out much either; he had his own bag of paperwork he was carrying as he looked for the right apartment door down the dark hallway. We found the apartment and rang the doorbell. There was no answer, so we knocked, which then a Hispanic lady answered the door and with limited English said come in. The manager did most of the talking by introducing us and getting her ready to hear about this wonderful product and hopefully make a purchase of the machine. I pulled the parts out and put the Kirby together to begin cleaning while the manager kept her busy and continued to "break the ice" with her. We started in the bedroom to demonstrate on her mattress how dust mites are located deep in the fabric of her bed, that she was inhaling these dust mites during her sleep. In addition to the amount of dirt left over from her old outdated vacuum cleaner that still left dirt and dust in her carpets. I felt kind of intrusive in telling her how "dirty" her home was.

After the cleaning and the slick talk of the regional manager, he presented the coast of the Monster Machine. Twenty-five hundred dollars! ($2,500.00) No way in hell can this woman afford a machine vacuum for that amount of money, I was thinking to myself! $2,500.00 for a tenement single mother! My thought was that that amount of money is a lot of money that could be used elsewhere and would be better served elsewhere for the benefit of her family as a whole. As I sat there listening to the regional manager coerce the single mother, I felt my emotions rise to a level of discomfort and anger. My spirit told me to punch him in the side of his head, because he was pushing and pushing different payment options for her to sign her name on the dotted line. And although I wanted my first sale, I wasn't about to get it by any means. There's a level of ethics, morality, and humanity that should lead you to understand that not all "riches" in life come in the form of money, and that not "all money is good money." We left the apartment after an hour of trying to persuade the woman of the house to buy, but she decided no and like I thought couldn't afford it. We left the high-rise apartment without the sale of the Kirby, and I was content with that. We arrived back at the office, and I dropped the manager off and told him I would see him tomorrow. I had a sense of worth, now that I had a " job," but there was still something missing. The next day back in the Bronx office, I made phone calls and created an appointment list focusing throughout the areas of the Bronx and Westchester, New York to sell my Kirby vacuum. I headed out into the New York streets with enthusiasm, a clean shirt, and my Sunday morning church suit hoping to sell at least one vacuum. Unfortunately by Thursday of the week, I had no such luck, and by Friday I had no sales. I informed the regional manger that I would not be back Monday.

CHAPTER NINE
The Second Scene

Since the Kirby vacuum days, I have had a few sales positions, which I did very well and was able to convince people and institutions to do business with me. However, at that moment in my life, I was young, undisciplined, and impatient for success. I was just coming off the field making thousands of dollars a week, to waiting on a paycheck of a few hundred dollars, and that wasn't sitting well with me.

This is how God's plan works. The supreme wisdom and power that governs humanity knew what was in my heart and knew what I needed to experience as I continued along this journey called life before my journey would end down the road. Within a week I received two calls, one was from the Miami Dolphins of the NFL and the other from the new Arena Football League. I was referred to the Miami Dolphins by my high school Coach Harold Crocker who was still at Iona Collage coaching football and had built personal and professional relationships in the NFL over the years through his integrity, commitment to his players, and his love of the game. I was grateful for his assistance in providing me with an opportunity to continue to live my dream on the gridiron. Arena was in its first year of existence with the previous year being an exhibition year. So I would be part of the inaugural season of the Arena Football League. There was a conflict with the time however. Both Miami and the Arena League wanted me down in Florida during the same periods of time in June. The days overlapped by three, so I weighed the pros and cons of each and decided to go to Miami and give it a last go at it.

This is the turning point in my life when my thoughts and beliefs of professional sports changed, and I realized it was not an institution of competitive competition between superior athletes alone, but was also a multi-billion dollar business whose focus is to make money for the wealthy owners of these teams. Any disruption in the mechanism that's in place that would jeopardize the any final gains or shun an unfavorable light on the team or league would result in you being dismissed or not sort out at all. My situation was the first.

I called back the Player Personnel Director of Football Operations and told him that I accept the opportunity to come down to Miami. He welcomed me and wished me all the best. The contingency plan was that if I did well during the tryout, Miami would offer me a contract for the season. I was excited because I was still working out, I was still fast, and nothing could take away the intensity that lay in my spirit and soul. I was also told that if I did well and the offer was made, that I would be able to return home and retrieve more clothes so I could remain in Miami for the remainder of the summer and go straight into mini-camp. I thought that was a good plan so I packed a backpack with toiletries and one set of clothes and underwear. I figured if Miami didn't want me, I wouldn't be lugging around extra clothes for nothing.

I got to Miami on a *hot* Friday afternoon and was picked up by Dolphin staff who drove me across South Florida to a South Florida University. I thought I was going to the Dolphins stadium and to a nice hotel, but no. I stayed in the dorms with other rookies and some veterans who they brought in to try out as well. I came right in after the thirty-minute ride from the airport and met with the man I spoke to on the phone who gave me all the details of my visit when in New York. He was a short pudgy man with glasses who sat behind his desk as he greeted me with a handshake and welcomed me to the Miami Dolphins. After a few minutes of pleasantries about my trip into Florida and the call he received from Coach Crocker, he made sure to let me know that he "heard wonderful things about me." He then presented a player injury waiver so I could start practicing first thing in the morning. This waiver would release them of all responsibility if I got injured during my time before I signed on officially as a Miami player. He reminded me if I did well, that the Dolphins would offer me contract for 1988-1991. I was excited of course because I knew I was ready and that they would get to see me up close and personal tomorrow. I was driven over to the dorms on a golf cart by football staff to my room where I met other players who they brought in for the summer to evaluate. They had not yet sighed contracts but were practicing and working towards one. That night, as I walked around campus, I felt the heat of the South Florida breeze and the smell of the salt water roaring off the coastal south beaches. The whole atmosphere of Miami was mesmerizing to say the least. I was thinking to myself, would I get to see the great Dan Marino or Dan Shula? I didn't know, but at the moment all I wanted to do was to get that contract offer and enjoy this South Florida experience. When I got back to my room, I was introduced to my roommate who was a running back (can't recall from where) who gave me the rundown of the practices and the free time they had after practice. Some would head down to South Beach for dinner and others would just chill around campus and see what "meat" they could find. I stayed in my first night hoping there would be other nights to check out the "meat" or hang out at the famous and infamous South Beach.

The next morning I got up and followed my roommate and other players down to the field for warm-ups and testing. After warm-ups I was told to stand on the sidelines and watch practice until I was called over to do my testing. As I stood there and watched how the receivers and the defensive backs battled in one on ones, memories of me in mini-camp returned, which ignited familiar battles I had with Odessa, Mark, and Stephen, and nothing was different here in Miami. A lot of back and forth competitive jockeying, which always made practice more interesting and creating an atmosphere of camaraderie amongst future teammates. "Morrison, come here" is what I heard from across the field from one of the assistant coaches. My time had come for me to test and show what I was capable of doing. I slid off my nylon sweatpants revealing my black spandex shorts that I matched up with a white Nike t-shirt. I brought my Nike three-quarter high cleats and headed over to where the call came from. I was given instructions of the two tests I was to perform, as well as a ball skills evaluation. The ball skills evaluation was basically breaking on the ball from different angles and back peddling. One thing I knew for sure was that my back peddling skills were par excellent from being taught by Sonny way back in the summer before entering college football camp my freshman year, and my ball skills were just as good. What I needed to do was run to run a sub 4.7 in the 40-yard dash and I would put myself in a good position to get that contract.

I killed the ball skills portion of the evaluation as I remembered. I tracked down the ball and caught everyone at its highest point that was thrown my way. I felt fast and I moved through the different cone drills without any hesitation. After a forty-five minutes of ball skills and drills, the 40-yard dash was up next. I rested for 20 minutes, which I used the time to rest and stretch. Pulling a hamstring would not be a good excuse to get another chance on another day or them to keep me in Miami until I got better. As I was waiting to get called over after stretching, I stood up on the sidelines looking over to the assistant coach waiting for him to call me over to begin. As I stood there and raised my head up from doing a hamstring stretch, I felt someone standing next to me who I didn't realize was standing there before. As I readjusted my focus and focused on him, I said hello and realized I recognized the face. He wore a summer tan shade bucket hat with a Miami Dolphins symbol on the front. When I looked closer, I saw it was the Head Coach Don Shula! I thought my legs would fall from underneath me from the nervous jolt I was feeling, and when I finally mentally acknowledged who it was standing only an arm length away from me, all I could say was "hi." He looked at me and said, "You look good out there." I thought I would choke when he said that! I got a compliment from a legend of the game. I said, "Thanks, Coach" and turned back to the field waiting for the assistant coach to call my name.

It wasn't time to get overly nervous now knowing that Coach Shula was in the midst overlooking practice. A little nervousness is okay because it's a sign of anxiousness that wants to get out and let loose of some energy, and I was about to let it all out on the 40-yard dash I was about to run. As I lined up getting ready for my first attempt, two coaches had their stopwatches out to mark my time. This was a time in this world without electronic testing and "laser accuracy" systems to do the timing. Coaches relied heavily on eye and manual hand coordination. I got down in my three-point stance for my first run, as the coach said, "On your movement." I took a breath and waited for the extra breath to leave my body and relax to a steady rhythm. I took off and I felt like I was moving fast down the lines as I approached the 20-yard marker. I felt power and the Florida air skim over my face as I drew closer to the 40-yard marker and as I stretched across the line. As I crossed the line, I knew immediately I messed up at the end of the run.

When running a 40-yard dash, you must run through the line at the same speed. By stretching you slow your body's momentum pulling you through which can cause a loss of momentum and a loss of fraction(s) of a second. As I made my way back down towards the start line, Coach reminded me of that very thing: "Run through the line," he said. "Not bad, but you can do better." As I was setting up and readying myself to run for the second time, I looked over to the far sideline to see if Coach Shula was still standing overlooking the practice; he wasn't and I didn't see where he took off to. As I adjusted my Spandex, I got ready for my second run at the 40. I stayed consistent in preparation with the breathing and relaxing of the body. Now, I just needed to remember to run through the line and better the time I had before, whatever time it was. The coaches don't tell you until after it's all over, so that you don't focus on time, but more on performing you natural best. "On your movement," the coach said again and as I got ready. I was off again! As I made my way down the South Florida grass field towards the 40-yard line, 20,15, 10, 5 and finish, as I made sure I ran through the line this time. I felt better with the run as I walked back towards the coaches. I noticed them comparing the times on their individual clocks, so I asked one of them, "How did I do?" He didn't answer and said after I met with the Player Personnel Director again, the same one I met a day earlier, I would be notified of my time and next steps.

I wasn't allowed to practice with the team for the rest of day until I was officially signed or just sent home packing. So I spent the rest of my time watching the receivers and defensive backs in their individual groups and walked around the field for the next twenty minutes or so. Practice was finally called up as the sun was coming down and the evening Pacific breeze blew from across the field. After the final huddle broke for the day, I was told to go see the Personnel Director to get my evaluation and what the next steps would be if any. When I got to his office, he told me to take a seat and "let us see what we have here." He got right to it and said, "You did good on the ball skills and field drills, but your 40-yard dashes were okay, not blazing speed but it was okay." I wasn't sure how to take that, and felt that was a dagger in any opportunity to get signed that day. He then says, "You did good enough to get offered this contract" as he pulled out a contract for me to sign. I was full with joy and excitement that I was going to be a Miami Dolphin, and I proved again that I was "good enough" and had the skills necessary to play in the National Football League. As I sat there looking over the contract, I thought I needed to contact my agent Rich Glickel to tell him the good news and get the okay to sign the contract. He congratulated me and reminded me to ask if I would be able to return home and retrieve my things and return Sunday night or Monday morning for practice. I nearly forgot about that "promise" the director made before I came down. I asked the personnel director when I hung up with Rich, "Can I return home tonight and get some clothes for the summer because I don't have any?" The director said, "No, we need you here first thing in the morning for practice." I was confused and felt tricked, because I was told I would be able to do so. I digressed and thought that since I was in hot South Florida, I wouldn't need much clothes in the middle of the summer anyway, and with my summer check I could always buy some shorts and shirts. Then I asked him about compensation. I was told I would get paid $500.00 per week, but out of that, I would be responsible for my own food and housing and any clothes I wanted to buy. Housing? All the players that stayed in the dorms paid rent? I wasn't comfortable with what I was hearing and what was happening to me in real time. I thought to myself, "Is this the side of professional sports people don't see?" Yes it is, the broken promises and the compensation battles between management and the players. For the first time I understood why players strike and requested large sums of money they believed they deserve.

I told him I had to think about it and would let him know. He was puzzled that I had to consider the offer, because most young athletes hungry and as a last resort to play in the NFL would jump at any opportunity to play and would have signed on the dotted line as soon as the paper contract hit the table. I didn't think that way, and although football was important and a big part of my life, and the possibility of changing my family's trajectory as well as providing for London and Kandice, I felt I was at the will and control of some man and organization that would determine my immediate fate in providing for them. I wanted to be in control of my life, my money, and how to spend it both. So I politely declined the offer as I returned the contract to his desk. He said, "Agents do this all the time, giving young players bad advice." He didn't know I assessed the situation myself after asking a simple question about a promised made and broken. He said I could spend the night but would be flown out tomorrow afternoon. When I left the office and headed back to my dorm room, I ran into some of the players and they said, "You looked good out there; did they offer you a contract?" I told them yes but I didn't tell them what my decision was. I enjoyed the moment and time spent in the last twenty-four hours, and they invited me out on the town with them. Saturday night in Miami South Beach sounded just the thing I needed, but after my contemplating my decision and conflicting conversation with the Player Personnel Director, I just wanted to go home.

CHAPTER TEN

I wasn't back home in New Rochelle but a week when I contacted the Arena League representative and told him I was available to participate in camp if it the opportunity was still available. The player representative wanted to know what happened in Miami, and that he heard I was in Miami for a "tryout" and why I didn't give an initial confirmation to my participation in the camp. I filled him in with parts of the particulars of why I left Miami, mainly around "contractual differences, " but I was ready to come down to the open tryouts in Orlando.

When I got there on Wednesday, I was already two days behind, and players from all over the country were trying out for this "new" football league, which was to begin its full regular season schedule. Of course on the day I arrived, I headed straight to the field in the midst of a downpour of rain, which led the field a muddy mess. As a defensive back, playing in the mud isn't he best conditions to break out and up on a receiver. Once again this is a time in sports history when not all universities or schools were fitted with artificial turf fields. Well there would be no excuses now. I left the Miami Dolphins discontent and disappointed looking for fairness and opportunity; so being in Orlando in spite of the weather conditions was my last shot on keeping the dream alive.

The routine was the same, get in line, stretch, then break down into your position groups and go through the drills. I recall I was slipping everywhere because the field had turned to mud under the downpour of the Florida sun. In addition, the conditions were made more difficult because this time I didn't bring along my trusty Nike high top cleats. Instead I brought my Nike low-cut turf cleats, thinking the grass would be dry, my feet would be lighter and would feel more like the surface in New York, where I used them while with the Giants. I believed that since Arena football was an indoor game that I would be practicing either on an outdoor turf field or indoor turf field. That wasn't the case, and my total performance wasn't up to my standards and the coaches didn't see me at my best performance. I looked around and saw others that I knew; Lovelady and Bennett were there trying out too. Both were in the Giants camp with me and crossed the picket line as well. They were two years older than me still living their dream of playing football and making some money before hitting the real world roads. Bennett had made himself a little name for himself for making the incredible catch off the back of a defender during the San Francisco game. That gave him some recognition during the camp as I witnessed coaches talking to him about the catch throughout the day. It was a one-day tryout with meetings at night as a follow-up and details about the league, the rules, and how the game itself is played.

Any time to redeem myself was all gone. Whatever I did this day would have to do, which consequently had me seriously considering getting a real job and supporting my new family. Kandice's patience was wearing thin. She wasn't able to work full-time in the salon, but she made a few appointments with clients in the new home around the corner from where her family lived in the same neighborhood. I had to make something happen, and it had to happen quick.

The next morning we all flew out of Orlando to our perspective cities and gave salutations until we see each other again. I headed back to New Rochelle and waited for the phone call from any team, but specifically from the team out of New York, the Knights. During this time, I travelled between Connecticut, New York, and New Jersey, where I spent time with friends I met while with the Giants and at home with the homies. I told Icky and Angelo what was happening and they were supportive and knew or at least understood the chances and the politics of sports. Icky was like, "Fuck it, man, if they don't call you, fuck 'em, keep it moving." Icky didn't let things worry him in life. He lived life to the fullest, every day and all day. I really appreciate that about Icky and his perspective and having that particular attitude towards life. Because sometimes in life you just have to say, "Fuck it!" I took a ride up to New Haven to see London and Kandice. At this time, our relationship was still intact but rocky. She needed me around to help with London, but I believed she knew I had to pursue this avenue of football with the hopes of landing a career in football that would help finance our future. I called home during the week to check in on my brother to see how he was doing. Michael was always doing something academic or keeping himself occupied. To this day certain feelings come over me that I neglected him as a big brother growing up. I knew the difficulties of being raised in the home without a father and with one who wasn't there a lot because of the separation from our mother. He also had a serious drinking problems that not only had an effect on me and my mother, but I didn't realize what I know now, and that is it had an affect on Michael too. Me not spending more time playing football in the back or playing catch with a baseball, or just sitting and talking with him or bringing him along with me to Coligni to hang with the fellas has had an affect on our closeness as brothers I believe. While I traveled back and forth up and down "the 95" or "the hutch exit 59" took away the opportunity to establish a brotherly bond that I wished for, even today. Let me be clear, the love is there for my brother. He has done so much with his life, in spite of our circumstances, which is a testament of his will and fortitude to succeed and achieve. During this time, Mom had just purchased a Tandy computer for him that he wanted. He worked on that computer doing things, which led him today as an engineer with a degree from University of Pittsburgh, which interestingly is the school our cousin went too and the one I wanted to go.

He was doing okay when I talked to him. He looked up to me and supported his big brother and wanted to play football too when he got older. I remember coming home one day and he had on my Giants practice undershirt and hat hanging out in the living room chair watching TV. He was and is a good little/big brother, and I try to make up for lost time that we didn't get to spend together growing up. Mom was home too and said, "I didn't receive any calls this week." It was already Thursday, and I hadn't received a call from the Arena League and the season was to begin in two weeks. At he time I didn't know what that meant, but I just took it as it being a new league and the protocols and communications were still being worked through. I decided to come back home during the week of the second week in case I would get a call and

I would have to get on the first plane out of New York or have to show up at practice somewhere in New York.

I didn't get the call, and the season was to begin the following weekend. I was upset which also meant that I didn't take advantage of my opportunity in Orlando and left an opportunity to play in Miami three weeks earlier. I felt like a failure and embarrassed that my credentials as a top tier football player was now tarnished. The narrative in the sports world is "You are good in college, but did you get to the league?" Although I had already played (and got paid) by the Giants and was currently in all Giants literature, my longevity in the league still leaves an empty space. My skill, I believe, wasn't seen by all, and I believed, even if it's in my own head, that I was one of the very best to play the game. But now, I'm home in New Rochelle and I can't even make an Arena football team. The week was coming to an end and the first game was to be played at the Knights' "home field," Madison Square Garden. The Mecca of championship sports, and this time I thought I wouldn't get a call to play until the second game (Knights won their first). And then, something happened during the first game; one of the starting receivers/DBs got hurt, and by the next day I got the call from the New York Knights to report to William Patterson College, in Wayne, New Jersey, to join the team.

Yes I was excited! It meant my football career and dream would continue for at least another nine games and put a pause on looking for a worldly J.O.B.

When I got there, I reported to conference room in the gymnasium to sign my contract and settle into my new digs. The team was housed in a local motel. I shared a room with an African American wide receiver from a Midwest D-1 school and for the time we were there we got along great. Playing for the Knights was one of the most interesting times of my career where I got to see another side of being a professional football player, the good, the bad, and the ugly. Some of the good was that I was still playing in a professional sport for money and I'm grateful for the opportunity to do so. The bad, which I will go into later, confirmed my position that the business of professional sports, favoritism, and bias exist. The ugly was when my anger raised its ugly head again and reviled the bottled-up pain of the journey to this day and the experience of the journey during the season is real.

The next day was practice were I was fitted for my equipment. I then made my way out to the field wearing my new number twenty-eight and my new position was wide receiver and defensive LB/DB. This position is played one arm length off the inside, back side of the defensive tackle. My responsibility is to cover the lone running back in the backfield if he goes out on a pass and help on run support. I was greeted by old friends from the Giants too: Crocicchia, who would be the Knights' quarterback, and other teammates Lovelady and Bennett at the wide receiver positions. They were happy to see me, and so was I, as we all felt at home together and ready to play ball. The next game coming up was on Friday night at The Garden and I would be starting at the position that was vacated by the injured player I replaced. I was ready and couldn't wait to get started. Usually, before professional games, players are taken away and placed in a secluded hotel where fans will not have access to and where coaches can monitor the movement of players after curfew. With the Knights, the players stayed in our rooms, but there was very little monitoring by the coaches, which opened the door to opportunities for anything and anyone making their way to players' rooms and extending the night's "activities" long after the lights should of been out. Luckily for Arena players, our games were played at night, so players had plenty of time to recover before the night's game. I can't recall who we played, but I was ready and whoever was on the other side of the line of scrimmage was going to get it. After the opening ceremony and the introduction of the founder of the Arena League, Jim Foster, we kicked off to the opposing team. We were on defense first which was good, which allowed us to get rid of any butterflies early. My boys Icky and Angelo were able to attend the game, and I could hear Icky in the stands yelling, "Kick his ass, Pat." All I could do was laugh and embrace his love, brotherhood, and friendship. Icky has always been there for me, protecting me, supporting and encouraging me on how to play the games of life and football. I knew Mom and Mike were watching the game as well as well as the folks back in Connecticut who I told I was playing in the Friday night's game, so I was ready. Defense went out first, and with a sense of urgency and intensity I began to make tackles close to the line of scrimmage. I was in a lot of the running plays, mainly because of the type of game arena football is. The field being condensed to fifty yards long and 28 yards wide doesn't leave much room to run around and extend plays. As a running back and blocker, you have to get up into the hole quickly and make a good block, and run north to south. To me, I was right at home in the midst of the madness making tackles and making plays on defense. When I got on offense, Croc threw me two quick slants passes, which I caught for first downs as we moved the ball down the field.

On offense, we had a few explosive players that made a difference on the field for us. I mentioned Lovelady and Bennett who both had NFL experience, but we also had Vince Courville who played for Coach Gerry Glanville's "Mouseketeers" and Jim Kelly of the USFL's Houston Gamblers and Dallas Cowboys of the NFL. Vince Courville was small in stature at five foot eight and one hundred and seventy pounds, but he was quick and fast and became our touchdown and kick return specialist. He scored our first touchdown of the night on a punt return, which brought the defense back out unto the field immediately. Defense was my specialty of course, and being back out on the defense just motivated more to find a reason (good or bad) to knock the hell out of someone.

We ended up winning that game, and I was awarded the Ironman Award for the best offense and defense player of the game. Some of the players celebrated amongst themselves back at the hotel, but for me, returning after ten o'clock and after such passion and intensity of the night, I was too tired to enjoy the moment, so I went to my room, cut on the TV, and fell asleep. The next morning, just like the NFL schedule, we had morning film, which I was anxious to see. When my play came up, the guys and coaches whew-ed at the viciousness and crushing hit I made and then asked me, "Are you alright? You angry about something?"

"Yes I was," I said to myself. I didn't know why. Was it still my experience with Aunt Louise? Was it watching my mom work two to three jobs to feed us? Did I feel I wasn't yet living the American Dream and providing a better life for my mother and hopefully my new baby girl? I had this inner anger that was and remains on the fringes of my emotions. In this case, the expression of my anger was embraced because it brought about the outcome we all were looking for. After film time we went through our morning stretching and walk through practice. After an hour of that we were off for the day. I spent the day hanging in the hotel in Wayne, New Jersey, which didn't have much for us to do and got on the phone and called home to Mom to see if she taped the game. She said, "I did," which meant I had a video to remind me of these days as a professional player.

We got paid that Monday too! The rule was, if your team wins, each player who plays gets an additional two hundred dollars in their paycheck. So after every win, any player that was activated for the game could walk away with a twelve hundred dollar ($1,200) check. I was looking forward to playing the next game because in my mind if I made enough money, I could add it to the Giant money to provide some financial support to my mother and Kandice. The week of practice went well, and the player I replaced was still out hurt with an ankle injury and I was getting comfortable and confident in what my responsibilities were and understanding the overall concept of arena football. We had another home game coming up, and I said win or lose I was going to rent a limo and head into the city and relax for an hour or so, watching the people and the lights of NYC. Saturday got here, and we played the team out of Los Angeles who had a former three-time Super Bowl Champion and Hall of Famer, Cliff Branch Jr. He would be the equivalent to Vince Courville as the offensive specialist returning kicks, punts, and a receiver. At kick-off again, Courville received the ball and returned it to the middle of the field. We were on offense first hoping to set it off like we did the week before. Unfortunately, what happened last game wasn't going to happen this time around. Crochicca threw an interception on the second play of the game, which was returned for a touchdown, and from that point on the game was down hill. We loss that game, everyone was upset and angry, and Cliff Branch scored two touchdowns. Some local friends that I invited left early, so I ended up driving around in the Manhattan by myself for the next two hours. When I got back to the hotel around two o'clock, the hotel was quiet; my roommate was sleeping. I took of my clothes, turned on the TV for a bit, then fell asleep around three o'clock in the morning.

After Sunday practice of walk through and stretching, we all didn't really feel like doing much. Some of us just hung around the lobby with friends and watched basketball, while others went out and visited with "friends" they met while living in Wayne, New Jersey. Tuesday came around and we were back on the field and the player that was injured earlier that allowed me to join the team was now back practicing. It's understood that a starter can't lose his position due to an injury, especially if the injury was a minor one like his was. So when practice started, the coached called him out to the starting defense. I felt funny not going out there with the first D but I understood. I was hoping however that because of my play and earning the Ironman Award for my play that it would be enough for the coaches to find a way to get me on the field somehow somewhere. As the season moved forward, we lost the next to games, and a few touchdowns were made by my replacement on the defense. He was an offensive player in college, and although he was talented, he was not defensive-minded and his tackling ability was not up to par. I recognized that I hadn't played for the next two games after he got back and so did other players and even the defensive coach. I asked him, "What's the problem with getting me in there?"

He said, "It's the head coaches' call" and that he doesn't know what to say. I felt my emotions rising and feeling that I was kept of the field for specific reasons—that I was black! It was evident that I was the better of the two of us, and winning the Ironman Award my first game showed I could contribute. It reminded me of the time back at Southern when Coach Gilbride didn't play me for Glen when we lost the first two games until they put me in and only lost one game after that.

The next game was a travel game away, and I was not going. I was disappointed and angry, but I held it in. I stayed back at the hotel, and although I could have went home and chilled with the fellas or even Connecticut, I stayed in my room and watch the game as we were getting beaten again. Lovelady, Bennett, and our front three linemen played well, but Arena being a fast pace game and a game of inches, you as a defensive player had to be quick to the ball and a sure tackler. But I could tell by Lovelady's demeanor on the sideline bench and from the camera shots of the bench that he was upset and wasn't saying nice things. I was boiling myself after watching the blow out of the Knights and for me not getting a chance to play for the next two games. We would see what would happen when they returned from the game.

When my roommate Stan came in after a late night, we didn't get a chance to talk, but in the morning I wanted to hear from him what happened. He said our defense couldn't stop the run around the edge and our offense couldn't move the ball. My roommate was a receiver that alternated in and out with Lovelady and Bennett bringing in the plays. That infuriated me even more, because the edge is the area to be sealed off by the linebacker position that I played and was now being played by an offensive player trying to play defense. I sat back and waited for practice to see what the plan moving forward would be for me, and the knights.

The day after a game practice was the same, beginning with stretching and light running, but this time the coaches were not smiling as usual, which told me they weren't too happy with the play from the team the night before. Even the general manager who occasionally attends practice was out there keeping a close eye on practice and asking the coaches a lot of questions about what they were doing. When it was time to run defensive plays, I wasn't called out on the first defense again. I couldn't understand why I wasn't being called! I proved myself to the coaches and the rest of the team that I could be asset to the team's success. I held it together as I alternated in a few plays to get reps and stay up on any changes in the defense scheme. As the weekend drew closer, I had a sense of anxiety and frustration building because I saw that my time on the field became less and less and the starter took most of the reps in practice. Friday came and the travel squad was chosen to go out to Chicago and play one of the best teams in the league. Chicago actually won the first Arena bowl game, and I wasn't chosen to travel again to play against one, if not the best offense in the league. I *lost it* right there and then, on the field, in front of the coaches and my teammates! It took Lovelady, Bennett, and a few other teammates to hold me back as I unleashed a flurry of expletives towards the general manager. I was angry and disappointed by the fact that I proved myself to worthy to play and start and if not start at least travel and have an opportunity to play and contribute to a team win. I felt like I was being oppressed and rejected. No coach came to me to explain anything other than what was told to me before, that is was the general manager's call.

Friday the team flew out of JFK airport on their way to Chicago. I wanted to play in that game too because one of my former teammates from Southern was on the team, Anthony Corvino. Anthony's a Long Island guy who was quiet but tough. He's a good person, a good man, and was a great teammate, and seeing him and competing against him would have been a highlight for me. Well, that was down the drain and just added to my frustration, anxiety, and anger. I sat home that weekend and watched us get smashed again. I didn't feel that bad by the end of the season, because Chicago ended up winning the Arena bowl again.

Everyone was down about the outcome of the game of course, but our losses weren't because we didn't have talent and a good team, but rather we didn't execute as we new we could offensively, and defensively not all the best players were on he field either. We were on the road the following week in Providence, RI against New England Steam Rollers, and I was excited about the opportunity to get to play, but I wasn't holding my breath based on how things were going and my outburst the previous week. I was hoping to get another chance because another former teammate from Southern was playing for the New England, David Henley. David was a year ahead of me and played strong safety in front of "Smitty" (another New Ro player) and was "put together" like a Greek god. I knew that when we'd play them, I would most likely be going head to head with him a few times.

I called home during the week to check on Mom and Michael. They were doing their thing, and Michael was planning on setting up the VCR to record the upcoming game for Mom. Mike was/is very technically minded, and what Mom couldn't figure out, he would. I also called Kandice to check on her. At this time our relationship had become strained, due to me not being around to support her and the pressures of being single mother with two children; my daughter London and her son from a previous relationship. I know it was hard on her, but us being young with different agendas, aspirations, and timeframes, it led to frequent arguments when we did speak, which often led to hanging phone up on each other, which left positions unresolved and me more angry going into the game. I knew this could not go on before or after the game and that something had to change for my own sanity.

Saturday would be here sooner than I expected, possibly due to a little anxious waiting to see if I would dress for the game or not. On Friday after practice is when I was notified by the defensive back coach who came to me and told me I would be dressing for the game and would be used on both sides of the ball and rotating mostly on offense due to the fact we were down me both on defense and offense positions due to injury. Whatever the reason was, I just wanted to play, and I knew within myself that I should be playing. I also realized again that many decisions that are made in sports are not necessarily based on personnel but rather on nepotism, business necessities, and dollars. I'm here now to fill a void and prove that I am an asset that gets results and not a liability.

Dave and I met briefly before the game at the center of the field. We were happy to see each other and talked about Southern football making it to the professional ranks. Dave didn't talk much but he spoke more than usual, which told me he was grateful to be out there playing the game he loved with me and making some money at the same time. The Knights kicked off to Steam Rollers, and we were able to hold them at their ten-yard line. The thing about Arena ball is that anything can happen on the kickoff because of the net being in play and the ball can bounce of it to any direction causing the returner to more vigilant and attentive to the kick and the ball to secure it before he tries to do something fancy or creative. The returner has to make sure the ball is secure first, even if you're only able to return it ten yards on a fifty-yard field. Our defense was out first, and my teammate from Kansas was out again and replaced with Lovelady who went out first on defense. Interesting to me that Lovelady would be placed at that position before me knowing that wide receivers play the corner back position on defense in the Arena League and not linebacker. I was able to play well again in he game catching three ball and big hits. One of the negatives about the game is that I suffered my first serious football injury in my entire career that was inflicted by Dave.

My shining moments would come when the opposing offense attempted to throw a screenplay to the lone running back, which was sent out of the backfield to the flat. My responsibility was to line up directly inside the defensive tackle and watch the running back and follow him during all running and passing plays. On this particular play, I recognized where the back was going and timed my hit to his chest as he caught the ball as he looked to turn up field for yardage. As I hit him, the ball flew into the air, his feet went up into the air, and we recovered the ball. As I looked down on him and telling him "not today," I saw that he was in pain holding his ribs and screaming. For a moment I felt concerned, but only for a moment because in a football game, in that moment, a player has no friends on the opposing team and the opposing team is your foe and enemy. I was delighted to see "my foe and enemy" in distress at the moment, as his team's trainer jumped over the padded wall and attended to him and assisted the running back to his feet as they made their way back to the bench, and stayed there for the rest of the game.

But in the third quarter, on an out pattern and catch, Dave got me back as he came up and laid a big hit on me into my rib cage. I felt a little twinge but thought nothing of it. I also felt a slight twinge in my lower back just like I did when I fell awkwardly when with the Giants. I jumped up after a few seconds, I felt good, and I ran back to the huddle. The adrenaline must have been on high because I didn't feel any pain in my ribs for the rest of the game. But after another loss, I now was in excruciating pain that required Tylenol, ice, and bandage wrap. Karma is a Mother.... I ended the season with eleven catches for eighty-nine yards, thirteen total tackles, and one INT. That was also the end of the New York Knights because at the conclusion of a 2-10 season the Knights folded due to conflicts with league founder Jim Foster and team owners who by the way worked with former USFL franchise owner whose team folded as well, Donald Trump.

CHAPTER ELEVEN
LIFE

There was no big farewell party after the last game. Sunday after a brief morning meeting, we were told to gather our things from our lockers, we could keep our white jerseys, hand in our room keys at the front desk, and be out of the hotel/motel by noon. Travel arrangements were already made for those out-of-state players, but I stayed around with Lovelady and Bennett to keep them company and just talk. Bennett lived in Hamden, Connecticut at the time, which was the next town over from New Haven, where he lived with his girlfriend that he met while playing with the Giants. So we planned on catching up once we returned to the area and settled in and had some down time to get readjusted. Unfortunately, that never happened. A few months after our return to Connecticut, he murdered his girlfriend by cutting her throat. It was reported that she threatened to leave him now that his professional football career was over and his "finances" weren't the same. Bennett spent many years in jail for his crime but not life. He has had no previous criminal history or personality issues and therefore his defense was temporally insanity. I remember sitting in my living room back in New

Haven watching the news when I saw the report. Watching him being escorted by New Haven Police into the police station, I could see in his eyes that he was not the same person I knew. He walked across the screen with an unsettling grinning effect on his face that was not Bennett at all. He was the calmest, nicest, and engaging teammate. I would never think of him committing such a terrible crime.

Lovelady was from Memphis but was heading to Atlanta. He gained employment with Morehouse College in admissions and currently owns a fitness company and trains track athletes. Me? I wasn't sure what I was going back to in New Haven and do. I drove my Toyota across the GW on "the 95" and got off in New Ro. I spent about a week with Mom, Dad, and Mike and made my rounds around the neighborhood before I headed up the Hutch to exit 59. First I had to say good buy to Icky, Coach Crocker, Angelo, and Al's, where I frequently went to get a cut before I left. Icky's farewell was a reminder to me was that I got ran over on a play during Arena ball. I don't remember any of that, but Icky considered any tackle that you don't put the runner on *his* back is getting run over and a loss. Icky kept it real and kept you humble knowing that there is always room for improvement, and if you're from New Ro, you're the best and you can do it.

When I returned to New Haven in late middle to late November, Kandice and the children were settled in a new home in the neighborhood. Kandice always kept a tidy clean home, and I didn't worry about the conditions in which London was living in. We tried over the next couple months to rekindle the fire we had between us, but the time apart fostered some resentments in the relationship, and that once burning flame was slowly diminishing out. I wasn't ready to hit corporate America yet with my communications degree, but my untapped passion to help at-risk youth was just being tapped into at the same time. I got my first non-football playing position working for a local youth program called Youth Continuum, in New Haven. I was lucky to get it. If it weren't for the help of my former roommate Stevie (AKA Keke) McCray who vouched for me, it would have been a little longer to get something. He worked there and he knew I was back in town and looking for something to keep me busy and bring some money into the house. The position was as a youth residential counselor, overseeing residence and teaching life skills in a supervising capacity. The house was about a mile down the hill around the corner from the house, so it was perfect location in my attempt to reconcile the relationship between Kandice and me. I worked there for a few months into March and April when I came home after working an overnight shift when I walked into the bedroom and found a letter written to me by Kandice on top of the dresser draw. It was three-quarters of a page that basically expressed Kandice's decision for me to move along and that our relationship had ended. She mentioned she had other interests and that I had until April to move out.

My heart was broken, and I felt less than a man, not being able to support or love the woman enough the way she wanted to be love. I was young, and my daughter was born out of love, so I thought that was enough. It wasn't, and I realize that a woman needs more than a warm body next to her at nigh;, she wants security, and at that time I wasn't providing it they way Kandice needed it. I moved out at some point and secured an apartment in North End of Hartford, CT. It was forty minutes away, but I was looking for other positions during my time at Youth Continuum that would bring in more dollars. As the months came and went, I started commuting from Hartford to New Haven for work. I often dropped by at night right before bedtime for London just to say hello and wish her good night with a kiss. One night heading from Hartford to Hew Haven, I drove by the house around ten o'clock and noticed the lights were still on, so I believed everyone was still up, since it was the weekend. I knocked on the door a few times, and it was eventually opened by Kandice's son, who was still in elementary school. I asked him where his mother was and where was his sister, my daughter? He said his mother wasn't home and that my daughter was upstairs sleeping. I didn't want to disturb London so I left and told the little boy not to open the door for anyone and left and went to work around the corner down the street. I called the house minutes later as I got anxious but there was no answer on the phone, and consequently I got worried. I left work and went back to the house. When I got there, Kandice's son opened the door with his sleepy eyes and said, "Mom not home yet." He didn't realize I just left minutes earlier, so I sent him to bed as I stayed in the living room and waited.

As I sat there waiting, I heard Kandice's keys jiggle as she opened the door to the duplex home we once shared. By now my rage was overflowing, and all I thought about was pain, the same pain I lashed out on the football field. I couldn't be restrained, and my rage was expressed through the destruction of property and violence towards Kandice as she sat there frightened. Her son heard the commotion downstairs, and unknowing to me at the time he had called the police. When the police arrived, I wasn't sure what would happen to me. I was not the renter of the home, and I didn't live in the home. A "domestic disturbance" call was not a good look for me to be in, but at the moment, my emotions, pain, and inability to show restraint forced me to lose control. As I reflect on the social climate of present day responses to domestic calls and the unfortunate outcomes of black men by the hands of *some* police, this particular night could of ended quite differently. I commend those police officers that responded that night by looking at the totality of the situation and provided advice to both of us, who were young, in love, and still had a lot of growing to do. I was sent off to return to work by the officers as they stayed behind and spoke with Kandice in her home. I thank her for not pressing charges that night, because this journey could have been documented by someone else or even worst, have a total different ending to the story.

During this time of transition for me, I started to realize that "real" life had taken a hold of my destiny and that I needed to start making some serious moves in my life. The first thing was to get my mother out of the "rat infested apartment" on North Ave in New Rochelle and into her own. I still had some money in the bank and pay stubs from a few months back from playing football that I could offer as proof of salary. Although the season was over and I wasn't getting paid anymore, the bank took the stubs as security and believing I would be returning to that field of employment. I was able to provide the down payment for the house, and within one month, Mom was able to move out of the apartment and live her dream of owning her own home in America. After that, I secured another job and first corporate position as a sales representative with Southern New England Telephone Company, selling MERLIN phone systems to local businesses throughout the Hartford, Connecticut region.

I was also getting pretty serious with Desiree, a young and beautiful woman that I met during my transition traveling back and forth from New York to Connecticut. We weren't able to spend much time together initially to get to know each other because I was still trying to work things out with Kandice. I held onto her number and called her up one day and asked her if she wanted to hang out one of the few weekends I had available between having London for the weekend and traveling to Mom in New York. Desiree was aspiring to be a lawyer and was preparing to take the LSAT exam. Consequently our time was limited due to our own agendas and responsibilities. Although I was working and making some money, I wasn't content with the salary I was earning. I was used to making thousands of dollars per week, to now making the equivalent to that which now took a whole month of work. I wanted to make more, and so I searched out for other opportunities in the Hartford area. "Where could I make a six-figure income to replace the six-figure income I was missing playing professional football?"

I took the State Test for the Department of Corrections. I was initially worried about working in a jail, but over the years I grew to understand what the plight of young, misguided, and under-educated black men ended up, and I believed if I worked in a jail I could or would be a positive voice and image for those who were willing to listen and watch me. And as for the needs of London, they grew weekly and monthly. Me waiting and trying to establish my independence as a man and the lifestyle I wanted to live, couldn't wait to climb the corporate ladder to get what I aspired for and become. What I aspired for was what I needed and what I needed is what I wanted, now!

For the next couple of months, I would keep in contact with my agent Rich who continued to look for opportunities for me to continue playing the game that I grew to love so much. While he did that I was able to secure a position in New Britain, CT at a school working with behavioral challenged children. It was my first encounter with children that suffered from trauma, mental illness, or were victims and casualties of experiences in their family ecology systems. I worked there and spent time my limited free time studying the history of Omega Psi Phi Fraternity, Inc. When I was at Southern, a few of my teammates were members of this fraternity and had a certain way of carrying themselves. Van Clive Johnson, Melvin "Big Bitch" Wells, Mike West, and Michael Jefferson who I mention in my previous book, *Before Common Ground, Living the American Dream. Journey of an American Football Player*, were all influential in one way or another of who I later became as a man. I wanted to know more about this organization with the hopes of having the privileged to join its brotherhood. So I spent any free time I had studying and reading books as part of my "Me time." I was now working two jobs hoping to live and provide financial support for Kandice. I was waiting for the State of Connecticut position to come through so I could stop working two jobs to make the money I wanted and just work one with overtime to make the money I wanted again. I worked with the children for about six months when I received the call from the Department of Corrections. I was cautiously excited about getting the call because, for one, I wasn't sure what I was getting myself into working in a prison, and two, the status of my football career was not yet determined. After going through the background checks, which took two months to come back, leaving me on egg shells. I didn't have a record, but I was anxious to move on from the phone company and get back to making good money to take care of myself. In the mean while, I continued working and was accepted into the Lampado's Club of Omega Psi Phi Fraternity, Inc. The Lampado's Club is the initiation group that a potential "brother" is in before he is accepted into the brotherhood of Omega. This would take up a lot of my time through the study of the fraternity and the noble men who came through the journey to Omega in the before me.

After two months waiting, I received the call from the Department of Corrections with the report date, time, and place. I would be in the academy and pledging omega at the same time. A daunting task, but these were the two things I wanted to achieve at this moment in my life, so whatever it took and whatever it was, I was willing to take it on. In the academy, I got to understand the role of an officer. His/her responsibility would be to maintain the security of the incarcerated for violating the security of the community. My job was not to condemn, (they were already being condemned) but to be the custodian of their stay while in confinement. My pledge process started in November of 1989 and my employment was to start in January of 1990. In the academy was where I first saw the destruction of drugs and poverty coming together hand in hand. Ninety percent of the crimes committed by the incarcerated person were drug related by persons as young as seventeen years old, just barely out of high school age. It was heart breaking to see these young black men in these conditions and it was difficult for me to understand. I grew up in a rat-invested apartment, where living in the projects would have been better living than where we were, on top of the shoeshine store and next to the Army recruiting center. Mom worked all the time, leaving me to monitor myself and be disciplined enough to come home at a reasonable time at night or the door would be chained up. My conditions were not as bad as some of these men, but some of these boys and men had it better than me. So what happened to me that shielded me from this possible reality. I believe it was the love of America and the projection of greatness that it provided anyone and everyone that wanted to live out their dreams and aspirations. When I got here in 1974, my dream was to play American football after watching the Steelers beat up on the Dallas cowboys. So what happened to these men? I believe what I had growing up was strong support systems in my corner. Those strong supports came from coaches and friends that showed me tough love when I needed it, encouragement when I needed it, faith in me that I could do it and God's Grace to do it. Maybe these men lacked these same supports in their community, which consequently landed them behind the Connecticut bars of justice. So I am thankful to those friends, coaches and teachers who guided me and protected me, because if it wasn't for them, this could of easily been a different story about me with me on the other side of the facility doors and bars, not wearing the Corrections Officer blue uniform but the correctional inmate orange.

The next year and a half was the most trying time of my adult professional career at the time. Within a year a after completing the academy and was in full swing at the job as a Correctional Officer. I was in a few physical conflicts with inmates that really had me questioning my decision by getting into this field. I had my degree in corporate communications, I had a sports background that I could of pursued with ESPN or I could have just found another corporate job wearing a suit and tie. At the time I placed in the forefront to define my manhood, but I soon realized money has nothing to do with being a man and manhood, confronting tough times, overcoming those tough times and making sensible decisions that would benefit myself and my family.

I was still pledging in the new year of 1990. I was already six months in and still learning the principles of the Fraternity and its Aim. I spent many long nights in study, community service and many nights of Toil (Work) for the fraternity. It affected me a bit, in that I started to see the world differently and my role in it. I had to do more with whatever I had, and having money or not was the lesson learned. Pledging also affected my job. As a new Correctional Officer you are put on a six-month probation-ary period, and in that six-month period, you can only be late three (3) times. I had already been late twice by three and five mi-nutes to roll call, but that didn't matter, I was late. One day I woke up and I realized I had less than thirty minutes to get to work. I had moved from Hartford to Cromwell Ct, a little town outside of Hartford off interstate 91. My roommate was also my Pledge brother Greg who was an engineer at a company in Cromwell. I was scared, nervous, anxious and angry with my self for over sleeping from a well needed afternoon nap after a long night out toiling for Omega. I was asked to work second shift, which was the busiest shift, after working on the first shift, which was a slower shift I worked during my probation period. I hadn't ad-

hadn't received my passport yet in the mail and I started to worry. During the first week of March I got the call from the World league that a ticket will be waiting for me from JFK to Montreal Canada leaving in two weeks. I would be cutting it close but I was confident and hopeful the passport would arrive soon. Well, like I thought, the passport got there three days before I was too fly out. I didn't tell Kandice ahead of time because I wasn't sure if she needed me or not for London but when I knew for sure that I would be flying out, I called her and told her what I was doing and when I get back Ill take London that next weekend.

My birthday was on the twenty-first for March and I was leaving that following weekend. I spent extra days at the therapist with hopes of loosening my back more, and it worked, I felt much better. With less than five days to go, I received a call from the league stating that the tryout was moved to November. " November?" I said to the representative. He said there were some issues with arenas that were not finalized yet, and so they put an holt on everything. I was disappointed, because I was ready to go and my back was feeling better and I had worked things out with my job. After coming to grips with that set back, I concentrated my efforts on finishing my pledge period, hoping it would be ending soon. I continued to work, see London, mom and pledge. I completed the pledge process in April of Nineteen-ninety, and it felt like a heavy weight was lifted of my shoulders. But when I reflect on my personal growth during the process, I am thankful I did it and the instillation of values, ethics and responsibilities that would stay with me for the rest of my life "Till the day I die."

Over the summer, nothing really changed for me. I was now a working stiff, part of the real world workforce that worked shifts, collected a check and had two days to enjoy myself. I hated it because I wanted more and I wanted to play football. As the summer came to an end and we were heading into the cooler months, I noticed my back began acting up again and now; the stretching and physical therapy wasn't working as effectively as it did before. The therapist a young guy decided to try a new machine he bought that was helpful for golfers in assisting them in their rotation of the hips and back. The machine was on platform where I had to be strapped in by the feet, waist, shoulders and head. I felt between Robo Cop and Hannibal Lector of Silence of the Lamb. Once the hydraulics was released, it allowed me to rotate in various positions that would help to strengthen the vertebrae and the muscle around the area. I did this for two months, along with traction hoping for better and improved range, with a bright future ahead. But " Robo Cop" didn't work and my back was actually getting worse. I put off going to a doctor, which made it worse and the pain started to intensify and affect my job attendance. I accumulated a few Personal leave time and vacation days after probation, but not enough to take off for a week at a time. I told the leadership at the jail of my issue and when it first happened and they scheduled me to see one of state doctors. I was now less than one month away from the tryout and my condition was not getting better, but worse. I thought to myself that I would take pain shots before I was to and insure I had no pain during the tryout. The problem now was I wasn't able to train to prepare for November. I scheduled an appointment with a "Top Doctor" in Hartford. I was able to persuade him to provide a shot for me before the tryout, but I had to agree to him that I would continue treatment with him when I return. I agreed, and a week before I had to leave for Montreal in November 1990, I received a shot of cortisone for pain in my L4 and LV5 nerve area. It would last three to five days, which was enough time to go, come back and return to work by Monday morning.

I never traveled to Canada before. The little I learned about it was that Slaves would flee North to the Union States or to Canada towards freedom, and my Sister; Pauline's father (whom I don't know) lived there too. This was the first time I was to step on Canadian soil and I was excited to do so, even if it was just for a few hours. We were told to bring basketball or indoor sneakers because the facilitators of the tryout were expecting bad weather for the weekend. I was picked up from the airport and driven directly to the stadium in the midst of a cold rain shower. Breakfast of donuts, bagels, juices, tea and coffee was served. After breakfast our measurements were taken, height and weight, and after the preliminary stuff, we walked through to a stadium of empty seats, outside in the cold and into another building where we all gathered in a circle to hear what was next on the agenda. We were informed that the rain had picked up to a magnitude of a storm, so therefore we will be doing tryouts in the gymnasium where we were now sitting. I was saying to my self " that's not going to work for me." The likelihood of someone or a few of us twisting an ankle was high this day. I knew for myself that the footwork on a grass field is far different than that needed on a wooden shellacked gym floor. I also felt that this would probably be my last hope and attempt to play football with my back in its current situation. so I gave it my all and did my best with what I had and where I was.

I did the usual stretching and warm up drills by myself, this time no group stretching was coordinated. We where called over to brake down into our individual positions, and where I would first have the chance to test out my running on the wooden shellacked surface. If you ever played basketball, you then know the kind of footing you have, however in basketball, the speed in which you have to run and the angles you have to cut, are different and not as crucial I believe as it is in football. One foot away in basketball you still have your hands to make a play by stretching and jumping high, but in football, one foot away is like a forever mile, and if your timing, angle and speed is off, you will never make the play. After our position and group drills we gathered together with the wide receivers to do one on ones. I wasn't sure how this would work out because there were rolled up bleacher seats in the gymnasium too, which meant you couldn't really go full tilt towards the side lines or you'll end up colliding into them. It would be a tricky navigation between the floor and the bleachers. There were about twenty Dbs in line with me, which meant that each DB would get less reps to prove themselves. I remember going about four times on our first going around and before our first break. I had two Pass break-ups, which equaled fifty percent success rate. I needed to be around seventy-five to eighty percent positive cover success rate to be recognized. After our quick box lunch break, we went at it again and I remember going against this kid who was doing good throughout the day as I watched him go up against other DBs and challenging them, which he often came out on the positive end. I recognized early in the tryout that he would be a challenge for me too.

We were up next, and I was wearing these indoor Nike turf shoes that didn't quite work well on the shellac surface, but no excuses, I went at it. I played off at five yards deep, giving myself room and time to react to any deep ball or across the field throw. The ball was hiked as he made his way towards me vertically, when he put one move on me and broke to the sidelines. That's where I didn't want him to go because of the bleachers near by, but he did and I broke towards him, but my foot slipped from underneath me as I accelerate towards him losing any momentum I had to drive on the ball on the right angle to the sidelines. Even with that one misstep, I still was nearly able to break up the pass, but I missed it by a step. For some reason I found it humorous as I chuckled back to the line and I watched the receiver in glee that he caught the ball "over me"

There were only fifty-eight of us brought in totally. We were told that we were highly recommended for this day by scouts from throughout the league that we were the best available at the time for this new league throughout the US, Montreal, and parts of Europe. One of the interesting points about this process was that after these tryouts, the league was having team drafts in Orlando, Florida, the same place the Arena tryouts were. There would be 10-12 teams with one of them be in Montreal; one of the reasons the tryouts were there. After a half-hour of waiting around, the coaches came back and thanked everyone for participating and that the names they were about to read out would be the players they wanted to stay for further evaluation. After the first eight names called, I thought my time had come and so I started putting on my sweat jacket and was preparing to head towards bus. But right then my name was called at number nine and I was asked to stay while the other players were dismissed.

Those of us who were told to stay were asked to take an onsite physical examination to determine to move on to the next stage of the process or not. This is where it got tricky for me. Should I to be totally honest? Or should I hide my physical condition from them just to go to Orlando and continue the dream. Was my health worth the chance? All these thoughts rushed through my head in the few minutes before I was up to get assess by the medical doctor. I sat there in Canada, and after a few seconds, I thought to just go to with the flow and hope they don't ask questions about my back, but if they did, I would be honest. As I went through the physical routine, which started with my eyes, then my neck, then shoulders, "Have you had any surgeries on your shoulders or body?" the trainer asked. That was a safe question, which I happily responded with a jubilant true answer of "NO!" He looked at my knees and saw that there were no surgery scars there either. He said, "You look good, but let me ask you one last question. Do you have any recent injuries?"

"Damn!" I said to myself. Why that question now at the end of the evaluation? "Should I be honest or should I say no just so I can move on?"

Well I was honest and told him that I fell recently and hurt my back and I was on "a little medicine" to keep the inflammation down, and that I felt no pain, and I was fine. He looked at me and I looked at him and I knew right there that I was done. He said, "We'll give you a call." Everyone knows when you hear "we'll give you a call," it actually means don't wait up because it's not going to happen. We all loaded up on the charter bus and headed to a hotel where they put us up for the night and had us all flying out the next day. I made it back to work for Monday and second shift, and the life of a working stiff two days earlier, on the block, loud with adolescent testosterone filled criminals.

After a week back and going through the daily routine of a correctional officer, I was called down to the captain's office. This time I didn't know why, but the only thing I could think of was that I used a sick day for the Friday I flew out. The captain's was a dark skin, tough veteran of the criminal correctional system who had worked his way from frontline CO to senior officer in the facility under the warden. When I got to the captain's office, he told me to sit down in the chair in front of his desk as he stood behind it. He asked me, "Where were you last weekend?" I was surprised by the question, knowing that what I do on the weekends is my business unless I broke the law or something.

I told him, "I went out of town."

He said, "Let's be clear, you took a sick day on Friday to go out of town." I was saying to myself, "So what's the problem? It's my sick day." He said, "The facility received a call from an unknown caller and reported that you were not sick and that you were in Canada trying out for a football team; is this true?" My bottom jaw dropped as I listened and tried to slow down in my head what I was experiencing and what he was saying and to really digest what I just heard. Someone called in and told? He went on to say (in words) that he hopes this is not a regular thing, but because I had time to do it, he'll let it pass. He wanted to know if he could count on me as an officer in the facility because he thought I brought value and a positive image to the young inmates on W-2. I told him, "Yes, sir!" and I did go away for a tryout with the World Football League, but I don't think it's going to work because of the injury I have to my lower back.

"Whatever it is, you have to make a choice between being full-time here or full-time on the field," he said. I returned to the block and thought about what he said and the decision I would eventually have to make and God's intervention in my affairs.

For the next couple of months, all I did was work and travel between Connecticut and New York allowing bonding time between London and extended family. Mom would take London and Michael to church together on the weekends while I would be home resting or hanging with friends before I headed back north. Michael was doing great in school, getting awards for his academic achievements. I was and have been very proud of him. Seeing him relatively raise himself up as a man without me being around or his biological father who was still dealing with the disease of alcohol abuse and unpredictable behavior. But he was always there for his niece, trying to keep her company, reading to her, and showing her the way. But he was a boy and wanted to do boy things, and so his time too was limited. As time flew by between 1990-1991, my back got worst. The time spent at work got fewer and fewer because of my inability to stay on my feet for long periods of time. I also was very concerned with getting into "Code Blue" calls and I wouldn't be able to help my fellow officers. I had to make a decision to go out on workman's compensation. It was a tough decision, but it was one that had to be made for my long-term health. It was I difficult time too because it meant I would be living on less money because of my inability to do overtime. child support payments had begun as soon as I got the job with corrections, so the amount to be paid bi-weekly had to be met no matter what. I was still going to physical therapy and seeing the orthopedic doctor who gave me the cortisone shot for my trip to Canada. Unfortunately, with all the spinal steroid shots, traction, and the "Robo Cop" contraption, I wasn't getting any better.

1990-91 wasn't gong to well for me. I fell into a state of depression that took control of my mental status, and I was at a fragile place at this time in my life, and to make things worst, I was caught up in the crime of the decade! The Charles Stewart murders in Boston Massachusetts. One weekend I decided to visit Desiree at school in Massachusetts. Upon my arrival in the city of Cambridge, I drove around the school, through campus parking lots looking to park my 1988 Audi 4000. As I entered one of the parking lots right off Massachusetts Ave near her housing building, two unmarked cars pulled in behind me and cornered me in my car. At first, I thought it was some idiot not paying attention and rolled up on me that triggered the anger button; that was always ready to be pushed. As the plain-clothed male individual got out of his car, I jumped out of my car too to see "was up." I was quickly made aware what I was dealing with when the plain-clothed man flashed his police badge with his 9-millimeter Glock visibly in sight. I knew right then that this was a serious situation and I had to play it cool and follow directions, as we (black boys) were taught to do growing up. "No sudden moves, keep your hands visible at all times, and be respectful, yes sir, no sir." I did all that, as my heartbeat doubled time wondering what was going on, and what would be next in store for me. The officer told me to slowly come towards him while he asked me, "What are you doing here?" I found that offensive, because I was a twenty-three-year-old, college-aged man on a college campus, so asking me that question only left me to believe that I was dealing with someone that had some biases, conscious or unconscious, and I would have to be additionally conscientious of that, and not push any of his buttons that would force him to respond in anyway that would cause him to react with force.

I told him, "I'm looking for a parking spot to park." The look in his eyes told me that wasn't good enough. I then told him, "My girlfriend goes here, and I'm here to pick her up." That seemed to help ease the tension in his face as he asked for my driver's license ID. I presented it to him as he looked at it, looked at me, and looked at my ID again. I thought I would be fine since my license would show a New York residence and not a Massachusetts, which would confirm that I was here visiting the area. Not the case. I was told to get out of the car and come with him where his car was, which the back end of his car was slightly hedging out unto the walkway. There he told me to sit on the curb. I sat there on the curve as he took my license with him into his car and called it in to the local department. As the initial officer was taking control of the situation, the back up officer was keeping a watchful eye on me with his hand resting comfortable on his 9.

The intense emotions were running through my mind and spirit at that time became overbearing, and I got the urge to stand up and address the officer about how biased and racist he was for pulling over a young black man for no apparent reason and holding him virtually hostage for not committing a crime and parking his car on an Ivy League campus. As my anger grew, I turned to the officer "overseeing" me, when the other officer who had my ID was getting out his car and heading back over to us both. He handed over my ID and said, "You fit the description of a suspect in a local crime."

I asked him, "What he look like?"

He said, "Tall, six-foot black male, mustache, short black hair."

"That's it?" I said to him! That could have been any black man in the city of Boston who met that description.

He said, "You're free to go." My blood was boiling, but I felt relieved that the situation was over and I was free to park my car and be on my way. Pulling me over as a black man, I found out later would be the description given of the suspect in the murder of a white pregnant tax attorney woman, which was the impetus of the citywide search of her soulless killer. After a few weeks of somber remembrance of the lost lives, the brother of the husband came forward as an accomplice in getting rid of the body and told the police that his brother, her husband, Charles Stuart, was the killer of his wife and unborn child. Charles Stewart knew that race in America was still a divisive mechanism that was one-sided and that oftentimes favored him because of his white male privileged advantages. He knew race continued to divide America, and if he used the "black man did it" card, those in power would not second guess to look at anyone else in the dominant culture as to who the suspect or suspects would be. If it weren't for the guilt of his own brother, it is quite possible that there could be a black man in jail today for a murder he hadn't committed.

I turned away with my ID in hand and walked towards the class buildings to meet Desiree, when I ran into Charles Ogletree, the tenured professor at the school who I had seen many times and ate lunch with once. I told him what happened to me at the parking lot, and he said, "Keep your head up, young brother; the fight continues."

My emotions and instability continued to move in a direction that I felt unfit to endure much longer. Who knew that just a few months earlier I was making so much money to now, unable to walk, unable to stand for long periods, unable to work because of my back had gotten worst and now I was out on workman's comp, and now, Desiree and I were on the verge of braking up. So many things were going on because of the distance between us, and there was nothing I could do to move the needle. I was determined to get her back, but I didn't know how, but I was determined. At the moment, I didn't want to be a burden to her with my issues while she studied to get her law degree, which was no easy task at the premier law school; plus, how useful would I be or could I be with a "broke" back. I didn't think she wanted to see a broken young man popping up at her door trying to court her, when knowingly she had many more "healthy" options in law school.

I moved from Cromwell, Connecticut to Hartford, Connecticut into a second-floor apartment of a friend from college's mother's house. It was roomy and it was mine. I stayed there alone for a year, and during that time, I continued rehabilitate my body. My depression grew deeper, as I realized that my career had finally come to an end. I was now unable to walk without assistance. Whenever I had to move from a sitting position to a standing position, there would be excruciating pain from the middle lower back down the backside of my left leg. This pain is called "sciatica pain," and although I felt a slight twinge previously, the pain and the severity of my injury had now become unbearable. I stayed in my new apartment alone for an entire year, coming out only to get London to bring to Mom's to maintain that connection. And while there on visits, I would remain laying on my back or on my stomach with Mom's hot red water bottle. But once back in Connecticut, my interaction now with my friends, fraternity brothers, and Desiree were limited to an occasional visit here or there during any given month or so.

CHAPTER TWELVE
THE FINAL WHISTLE

By 1992-93, I moved back home to New Rochelle to continue physical therapy and save some money. I settled with the state of Connecticut for a five-figure settlement, which at the time I thought was reasonable. I realized later that the lawyer I obtained had worked with the State of Connecticut for many years and was known for settling cases to free the State of any future legal action. As a stipulation of my settlement, I wanted the State of Connecticut pay for the surgery that I would eventually have to relieve the pain from my back, which was tracing down my left leg. It is called a laminectomy, an operation that "shaves off" some vertebrae in the spinal canal to relieve pressure.

While I waited and delayed the inevitable decision (surgery), I took a position at Mt. Vernon High School as a substitute teacher. I taught my favorite subject, History, which I grew to love and specifically African American History and the vital role Africans and African Americans have played in the development of the new world. As I reflected on the curriculum, I recognized much of what I now know and knew at the time about African American history was not in the history books passed out to the ninety-eight percent of African American urban high schools. This new critical eye that I developed over the past two years was due to the influence of Michael Jefferson back in my freshman and sophomore years at Southern. I didn't realize the significance of his direction, instruction, and example of how important and significant the American experience was and is to the African American, and now I had a moment to look at my own experience and views of America that warranted me to go back in time and relive my journey in America and evaluate, reassess, and make new conclusions. In some instances, the new conclusions were drawn from my Boston experience and current situation.

So my new insight to evaluate and reassess my perspective is what I intended to bring into the classroom of the 98% African American school I was now working in, which had a very high incident rate of violence and fatal incidences. I wanted to provide and present an image of success and content that would renew the students' minds, worldly outlook and consequently change their actions and behaviors moving forward.

The year was going well at Mt. Vernon High School, and the students gravitated to me because of my football background of course. I was one of two black teachers and that I played football at the crosstown rival, New Ro High. The rivalry between the schools was serious to a point where oftentimes it became dangerous to attend games at each other's schools or even walk the streets in each other's cities. The interesting thing about that dynamic was and remains the fact to this day, is that most families have family members in each other's cities, as well as attend events in each other's cities. But when it came to sports, football, and basketball, it was like war between the Catholics and Protestants during the conflicts in Great Britain. Consequently, my classroom experience was rewarding with student engagement, full with energy and excitement about the day's lesson.

Days and months had passed, and my back wasn't getting any better. I scheduled an appointment during the Christmas break with my doctor in Hartford, Connecticut to assess the severity. The pain was becoming overwhelming, and getting up in the morning to go to school became more and more difficult every day. Before I got to Hartford, I stopped off in New Haven to see Kandice and London. London and I spent sometime together before I had to get back on the road. London was about to turn four years old already. Time was moving, and I was still contemplating if I would continue the journey to an active roster in the NFL or if it was time to give it up. Well, I wasn't going to make that decision until I got to Hartford to see my doctor. When I got there and walked in the office, I was honestly nervous but hopeful the doctor could provide other options to help any additional services other than I had already tried. Before moving, I tried traction and spinal steroid shots; nothing worked. On this day I hoped Doc could come up with something, a treatment that would relieve the four-year pain I was experiencing.

Doc and I sat and reviewed health questions in the office; he did an examination on my back, then sent me down to x-ray. When I came back to his office after three hours, I was told that there was no change in my condition and that we would need to do the surgery as soon as possible. Doing the surgery would provide relief now and provide the quality of life I was looking for at the tender age of twenty-seven years old. I thought a lot about what was said, and I thought about what that meant. At twenty-seven years of age in professional football is the crossroads from being a young player and a veteran. I would be veteran if I returned now, and what kind of future would I have? My thinking was that I only needed to play one or two seasons of a six-figure income and then I could take care of Mom, Mike and London. I would be fixed with no pain, but would I get the opportunity. The mere mention of an injury already shut the door on one opportunity in Canada. But I had faith and would give it one more chance if given the opportunity. The surgery was scheduled for after the school year, so it would not be until the Fall 1993 before I would consider playing again.

As I drove by New Haven looking over the rails of the Merritt Parkway unto the Amity section of the city, I thought about London and what I wanted to do for her. I said to myself, "I can't have my baby want, when her dad is still here." I wanted her to be proud of me, and actually have her experience her father play the game he loved so much. I returned home and went straight to my room on the third floor and laid down wondering what would be next for me. Christmas had come and gone, and time was spent home thinking, stretching, and relaxing. All I had to do was finish out the school year, get the operation, and if it was successful, give the NFL one more try. That was the longest and mentally frustrating year I think I had ever experienced as a student or teacher.

While at Mt. Vernon High School, I immersed myself into the afterschool activities working with the school band, which was under the direction of Dr. Frank Able. Dr. Able was and to this day is one of the most prolific marching band conductors in the country. He is legendarily known as the band conductor of the legendary Florida Agricultural and Mechanical University

(FAMU) marching 100! He incorporated "Stepping" into the band's halftime shows to get more students involved in after-school activities. I was able to get a few boys involved in the step squad because they lnew girls would be there and I told them that boys who step impress girls. I told them when they get to college, they would have the opportunity to get a great education and enjoy the company of young women who like men that stepped. Some of the male students were on the verge of losing the race of life. It was easy to tell they were looking for a place of their own and a place to belong and someone who cared about their future. And because they weren't comfortable in their current space, many of them frequently acted out in defiance or delin-quencies, which put them at risk. I was able to "befriend" and build a relationship with one the male students. He loved football, but he felt he wasn't big enough to play the game for Mt. Vernon. I told him of my story and how many people doubted I could play the game and that I wasn't "big enough" too. After our conver-sation, he thought about trying out for the team in the fall. Until then he would join the step team to "see the girls" and give him-self something to do.

After a couple of weeks of practice in the gym and learning steps, we created a routine to be performed at the next home bas-ketball game. We were prepared for the upcoming game during the following week, but I noticed my "new student friend" was not at practice. When I asked the other students "if they have seen him", they looked at me as if I was an alien. "Didn't you hear, Mr. Morrison?"

"No what?" I said. " My "friend" was shot and killed the night before on the street corner while hanging out. My body didn't move.

I was frozen, and I felt like I was moving and listening to what I just heard in slow motion and muffled. This was the second student this month that was killed by gunfire from Mt. Vernon High School and there was nothing I could do about it. Mr. Able informed me that it'd become a common occurrence for him since he'd been there, and he hoped his ability to bring students into the band would help reduce the causalities of inner city life in Mt. Vernon.

When I went home that night and went to my room on the third floor and took off my clothes and laid my head down to rest. Mom wasn't home yet, but we had leftovers for dinner, which I didn't feel like eating at the moment, so I left it on the stove. I said to myself, "I gotta give it a go again, just one more time before I move on." A colleague at the high school and former opponent who played football at Mt. Vernon asked me to enroll with him into the Columbia University's teacher certification program. I thought it was a great idea, and I thought sincerely about it. He actually went ahead and enrolled into the program, but I still wasn't ready to move. So in March of 1993, I went in and had the laminectomy on the lumbar four and five vertebrae. The surgery was successful, and I was free of pain within hours after I woke up. I felt encouraged. I stayed in the hospital for another day before I was discharged and returned home to Mom's in New Rochelle. Mom being a Christian woman prayed for me during this time and was relieved that the pain was over. I could walk and sit without pain now, which allowed me to get back to work of taking care of my responsibilities in New Haven. A follow-up appointment was scheduled in two weeks back at the doctor's office in Hartford, but before then, I had to spend time with London in New Haven before heading up to see Desiree in Boston.

I arrived to my appointment on time and was excited to hear some good news and report that I haven't felt any pain since the surgery and that I've been walking to strengthen the area and prevent scar tissue from building up. I was doing every thing in my power to regain my ability to move and eventually start running. Doing this coupled with the doctor's positive report, if all went well, I would return to playing football again. I was called into his office and was directed to sit down in the chair in front of his desk. As he came in with a folder in his hand, I got up and immediately greeted him with a handshake. I wanted him to see my movement currently compared to how he first saw me months earlier. I was hoping my current status would heighten his diagnosis and say something that would be fitting about future recommendations.

He opened his folder and began to review my medical history and treatment. He reiterated again the surgery was successful and that I could return to normal activities as soon as possible. In my mind, that meant industrial corporate employment as well as a return to professional football. I asked him directly if I could return to football. He paused, as he looked at me with concerned eyes and raised brows. He looked concerned by the fact that I would ask such a question. The 90s was a time when the league was experiencing many head and neck injuries to players that caused them their careers to end. Even Scott Mersereau, my teammate from Southern who now was playing for the New York Jets, was in a incident on the field where his teammate ran into him during a tackle that consequently left the teammate paralyzed. The doctor lifted his head and looked at me in my eyes and said, "No returning to football, it's out of the question." He must have seen the reaction on my face and in my eyes, which was of disappointment. As he continued to lay out my instructions moving forward, I could see he was firm in his validation, decision, and discharge recommendations. He said, "If your get hit wrong again, you could be the next player to be paralyzed." Although his statement was heartbreaking and something I didn't want to hear, it made me realize the actualization and realization that my career as an American football player was finally over.

I walked out of the doctor's office at Hartford Hospital and looked up into the blue sky and took a deep breath. Oddly, I felt as if a heavy burden was lifted of my shoulders and that I was beginning a new life. A life of which was not yet clear, but a new start anyway. I was months away from marrying Desiree at this time. The relationship had bounced back, and she stood by me during the uncertainty of the time. She never wavered in her support, even though she was still a student and had not yet found employment herself. We were going to begin a new journey in life together, broke financially but healthy physically, mentally, and in spirit.

So although my journey to live out my American Dream of playing American football ended sooner than I wanted it to, I still have many more dreams to live out in America. I am thankful to God for providing my mother with the strength, will, and fortitude to live her dream too. Her dream of owning a home in America and giving her boys the opportunities to live out their own dreams too is the little hope that all immigrant mothers have for family kin. Along this journey in America as an immigrant football player and person of color, I have experienced many things that continue to haunt me today. The psychological effects of those experiences has kept the fire burning in my soul and leaves a constant uneasiness of fragility that keeps me frustrated, angered, and at times feeling hopeless for people that look like me. So as much as America has to offer, it too has much to atone and change the language in which it speaks to the masses that keep immigrants of a darker hue on the fringes of American society. America is the great experiment of "democracy" which is based in justice, which is fair dealing between its citizens. As such as we say it's the land of liberty for all, we must honestly ask ourselves, "As written in American history, has America dealt fairly with its darker hued population outside of sports and entertainment?" I would say no, and it is that fact that keeps me dreaming of a better America for all persons, and to relieve immigrants of color from the mental and emotional nightmare they experience along the journey.

That being said, the journey continues, the hope continues, the wishes continue, that the doors of freedom, justice, and liberty in the Hudson Harbor remain open and provide immigrants like me the opportunity to partake in the great experience of making this the greatest country in the world.